# HERTFORD COUNTY

## NORTH CAROLINA'S

### FREE PEOPLE OF COLOR

### AND THEIR DESCENDANTS

D1557382

Warren Eugene Milteer, Jr.

*For my grandparents,*
*and*
*in memory of Aunt Lennis.*

# Contents

# Preface

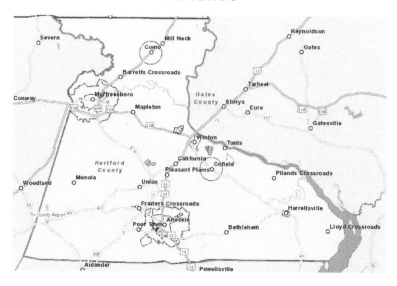

My interest in family history led me to research the history of Hertford County, North Carolina's free people of color and their descendants. In the late 1990s, I began to slowly piece together the genealogies of my ancestors from Hertford County along with those families closely connected to them. I quickly learned that the family tree that I initially set out to uncover instead was something more akin to an intertwining vine. The connections among families by the twentieth century were so mingled that it was nearly impossible to describe where one branch of the interconnected families began and another ended. An additional feature that I discovered about these families was the variety of mythologies about them: stories about their origins, their situation within the larger Hertford County community, and their general behavior. The purpose of this book is to explain and explore the more complicated experiences of these often misunderstood people.

# Acknowledgements

I am grateful for the assistance of many people who have helped bring this project to fruition. My research on Hertford County has taken me to several repositories around the country, and I would like to acknowledge their archivists, librarians, and other personnel. Past and present staff members at the State Archives of North Carolina, State Library of North Carolina, National Archives, Southern Historical Collection and North Carolina Collection at the University of North Carolina at Chapel Hill, the Moorland-Spingarn Library at Howard University, the Library of Virginia, the Pope House, the Rubenstein Library at Duke University, and the Joyner Library at East Carolina University have helped me procure documents and other resources. Several people offered editorial critiques or shared their invaluable family photographs, documents, information, and stories for this project including Shawnee Smith Ball, Angenita Boone, Celestine Combo Brickers, Wayne Brown, Flora Walden Chase, Marian Manley Chavis, Courtney Colligan, Robert DeBerry, Marion Reid Flagg, Cecil Goins, Pamela Graham, Barbara Archer Gregory, Frederick Gregory, Michael-Lynn Hale, Terry Hall, Joyce Harris, Kwame Hooker, Robert Hutchinson, Sheila Jones, Wanda Hall Jones, Undean Wiggins Jones, James D. Lewis, George Lima, Stephanie Milteer, Connie Brown Mitchell, Harryette Reynolds Morris, Alice Jones Nickens, Jacqueline Pastreck, David Powell, Reuben Price, LaVie Jones Pridgen, Marie Richmond, Ronald Robbins, Raymond Robinson, Graylin Simmons, Stephanie Sissler, Liz Myrick Smith, Avon Howard Stukes, Merilyn Weaver, Denise Wiggins, James Wilkins, and Carolyn Robbins Winston. I would also like to thank my family for their constant support.

# Introduction

From the colonial period into the twentieth century, free people of color and their descendants played a significant role in the social development, economic growth, and political life of Hertford County, North Carolina; they were not people living on the edge of society but people who helped to shape their community. As free persons of color, they held a general legal position above the enslaved masses and below the white elites. After the Civil War, some of them struggled for and obtained political and social power within the new order by serving in public office, gaining formal education, and becoming teachers and other noteworthy community leaders. Social success for these people during both of these eras, however, was largely dictated by the politics of gender and class. Throughout the period, men essentially excluded women from formal politics and limited their influence in other public arenas. In many ways, differences in access to wealth divided all Hertford County residents including free people of color and their descendants into the haves and the have nots. Even among this population, wealth, access to education, and connections to powerful elites placed them within a multi-tiered hierarchy.

Today, descendants and observers discuss and debate the ancestral backgrounds of Hertford County's free people of color. Most agree that people of Native, European, and African backgrounds were part of their ancestral milieu in one combination or another. Multiple historical sources provide support for these assumptions. William D. Valentine, a white nineteenth-century lawyer discussing the backgrounds of free people of color, explained that "free negroes are slaves and their descendants emancipated by Quakers and other benevolent whites and owners of them. The mulatto is the offspring between the white and the negro, or between the Indian and the negro, or between the white and the Indian."[1] When the

---

[1] William D. Valentine Diary, Volume 12, 164-165, Southern Historical Collection (from here SHC).

sociologist E. Franklin Frazier visited Hertford County in 1930, the former free people of color and their descendants classified their ancestors as "mulatto," "Indian," and "white."[2]

Many different families moved in and out of Hertford County over the years. Some appeared in the area before Hertford County was carved from Bertie and Chowan Counties in 1759. Others arrived in the vicinity during the late eighteenth century and first two thirds of the nineteenth century. Free people of color and their descendants tended to live in the eastern part of the county near the modern-day towns of Winton, Cofield, Union, and Ahoskie as well as in and around Murfreesboro. During the period between 1790 and 1860, Hertford County was among the North Carolina counties with the largest populations of free persons of color. Nearly one in thirty of the state's free people of color lived in the vicinity immediately before the outbreak of the Civil War. In 1790, the enumerator for the first federal census counted 216 free people of color out of a total county population of 5,828. By 1820, the free population of color had increased to 736 or 9.5 percent of the total population. In 1860, 1,112 free persons of color composed 11.7 percent of Hertford County residents.[3]

A relative lack of historical sources makes recounting a more complete narrative of Hertford County's free people of color and their descendants particularly difficult. During the nineteenth century, Hertford County suffered two courthouse fires that destroyed the bulk of the county's public records created before the mid-1860s. Many of the post-Civil War records also appear to be unaccounted for in the holdings of the state archives and the county register of deeds and clerk's offices. These record losses have left many questions about free people of color in the county unanswered. The residuals of the county's records provide few answers to queries about the connections between the region's indigenous people such as the Meherrins, Chowans, and Tuscaroras and the free

---

[2] E. Franklin Frazier Papers Box 131-92, Folder 7; Manuscript Division, Moorland-Spingarn Research Center, Howard University.

[3] *Heads of Families at the First Census of the United States Taken in the Year 1790 North Carolina* (Washington: Government Printing Office, 1908), 9; *Census for 1820* (Washington: Gales and Seaton, 1821), 112; Joseph C. G. Kennedy, *Population of the United States in 1860* (Washington: Government Printing Office, 1864), 358.

people of color and their descendants, many who claimed Native heritage. The surviving records also offer little insight into how all of the free persons of color obtained their free status. Free people of color were born free if their mothers were free or if they received their liberty through manumission, a legal process in which a master emancipated an enslaved person. Yet the surviving historical records fail to reveal which of these paths to freedom apply to particular families. Furthermore, the surviving records are limited in their capacity to tell us about many aspects of free people of color's lives such as their feelings and thoughts about particular events or even insights into their daily routines. As with many historical sources about underrepresented and marginalized populations, those records that reference free people of color often come from the hands of whites and are written from their perspective. Only a few records survive that provide us with firsthand testimony from free people of color.

This book is divided into four chapters, each crafted to convey both the consistency of the experiences of the people and the effects of change over time. The first chapter explores the colonial origins of Hertford County's free people of color and focuses primarily on their experiences during the eighteenth century. Chapter 2 examines the position of the county's free people of color in the period between 1800 and the eve of the Civil War. The book's third chapter investigates the dynamic changes that took place during the Civil War and Reconstruction for the people categorized as "free persons of color" before the war. The final chapter focuses on the experiences of these people during the Jim Crow period. A conclusion that illustrates the significance of this book follows the final chapter.

# Chapter 1:
# The Eighteenth-Century

There is no one moment in time that can truly be defined as the beginning point for free people of color in Hertford County. Native people lived in the region that would become Hertford County for centuries before Europeans arrived in the Americas. According to the surviving records, families considered by their neighbors as free people of color were present in the region that would become Hertford County by the 1740s and 1750s. A 1751 Bertie County Tax List provides the names of the free families of color present in the area during the period. They included the households of Thomas Archer, Henry Best, Joseph Hall, Gabriel Manley, Abel Manley, Littleton Manley, James Nickens, and William Weaver. The tax assessor described all of the members of these households as "free mulattoes." Along with a few others, members of these families composed the free population of color in Hertford County for the rest of the century. As per the 1790 federal census and other eighteenth-century sources, the families that joined them included the Bailey, Bass, Bizzell, Boone, Bowser, Chavis, Garnes, Keene, Orange, Reid, Reynolds, Sears, Shoecraft, Smith, Wiggins, and Williams families.[4]

During the 1700s, these families made important headway in the development of Hertford County's society. They did not affix themselves to society's periphery but actively participated in the community's daily happenings. As part of the community, they partook in civic projects, served in the defense of the county during the American Revolution, and labored as skilled artisans and lowly apprentices. In the courts, North Carolina law and local customs prohibited them from serving as judges or

---

[4] Bertie County 1751 Tax List, Colonial Court Records, Taxes and Accounts, Box 190, Tax Lists- Bertie 1751, 1753, 1754 Estate Tax- Beaufort Pet., n.d., State Archives of North Carolina (from here SANC); 1790 U. S. Federal Census, Hertford County, North Carolina.

jurors. Yet they still used the courts widely as defendants and plaintiffs in civil suits and criminal cases.

Before their arrival in North Carolina during the mid-1700s, many of these families had previously lived in Virginia; these families included the Archer, Hall, Manley, Nickens, Shoecraft, and Weaver families. Tax records show all of these families residing in Norfolk County, Virginia during the 1730s. Before traveling to Norfolk County, the Nickens, Shoecraft, and Weaver families had lived in Lancaster and Northumberland Counties on Virginia's northern neck. The waterways that connected the Northern Neck to Virginia's Tidewater and the rest of the greater Chesapeake Bay region likely brought these families to the Hampton Roads area. Records from Lancaster and Northumberland Counties suggest that the Nickens, Shoecraft, and Weaver families were already closely associated by the time of their arrival in Norfolk County. Leaving some of their relatives in Virginia, the families crossed the colonial border and continued south until they reached Bertie County. Into the nineteenth century, members of the families would continue to move back and forth between North Carolina and Virginia.[5]

On their arrival in North Carolina, the heads of these families purchased land upon which to establish their homes, outbuildings, and farms. In 1741, William Weaver had the Bertie County clerk record a deed showing that he had purchased 300 acres from Thomas Stevenson. Near the same time, John Archer acquired 200 acres from Stevenson. Into the next decade, other families from Virginia purchased additional land within the general vicinity. By the time the American Revolution had broken out, free persons of color owned over 900 acres in Hertford County.[6]

All of the landholding families would have farmed parts of their properties, and most of these families kept livestock. Joseph and Margaret

[5] Elizabeth B. Wingo and W. Bruce Wingo, *Norfolk County, Virginia Tithables, 1730-1750* (Norfolk: Elizabeth B. Wingo and W. Bruce Wingo, 1979); Nickens Last Will 1735, Lancaster County Wills, 1719-1749, Library of Virginia (from here LVA); A List of All the Tithables taken from Sugar Mill to the Great Bridge & So Up Both Roads as followeth for ye Year 1733, List of Tithables from Deep Creek to the Bridge and from Bridge to Northwest Landing 1736, Norfolk County Tithable Lists, 1732-1752, LVA; Tax List Hertford County 1779, General Assembly Papers, GA 30.1, SANC.
[6] Bertie County Real Estate Conveyances, Volume F, 319-320, 352, SANC.

Hall's assortment of farm animals included cattle, hogs, geese, turkeys, and a horse. Daily farm work on the Hall farm would have involved caring for these animals along with plowing the fields, planting crops, and picking the harvests at the end of the growing season. Additionally, Joseph Hall's estate included butter and churns, which suggests that an individual in the household milked the cows and converted the milk into butter.[7]

In addition to operating their farms, free people of color fed their families and contributed to the community by working as artisans or laborers. Gabriel Manly worked as a cooper or barrel maker, and Joseph Hall was likely a shoemaker as his estate included shoemaker's tools and leather. During the colonial and early national periods, county courts expected free men or their hands to construct and repair the local roads, and free people of color were often among the road crews. In 1754, county officials required William Weaver, Thomas Archer, John Archer, and Hancock Archer along with several of their white neighbors to work on the road from Alexander Cotton's Ferry to Deep Creek.[8]

Those free people of color at the lower end of the economic spectrum labored as servants and apprentices. During the late 1750s, the county court apprenticed several of Amiah Weaver's children to her white neighbors. In 1757, the court bound her daughter Lucy Weaver to John Campbell to learn "the Business of Spinning."[9] A little more than two years later, local officials apprenticed two more of Amiah's children to William Witherington. Witherington promised to teach her daughter Bridget Weaver "House Business" while Amiah's son John would learn the cordwainer's trade.[10] During their apprenticeships, North Carolina law prohibited the Weaver children and other apprentices from marrying or engaging in sexual relations. In exchange for their services, masters

---

[7] Tax List Hertford County 1779, General Assembly Papers, GA 30.1, SANC; Joseph Hall Inventory, Bertie County Estates, Box 35, Joseph Hall, SANC.
[8] Order for a Road from Cotton's Landing, Bertie County Road, Bridge and Ferry Records, Box 1, Road Papers 1751-1755, SANC.
[9] Lucy Wever, Apprentice Indenture, Bertie County Apprentice Indentures, Box 7, 1750-1759, SANC.
[10] Bridget Wever Apprentice Indenture, Bertie County Apprentice Indentures, Box 7, 1750-1759, SANC; John Wever Apprentice Indenture, Bertie County Apprentice Indentures, Box 7, 1750, SANC.

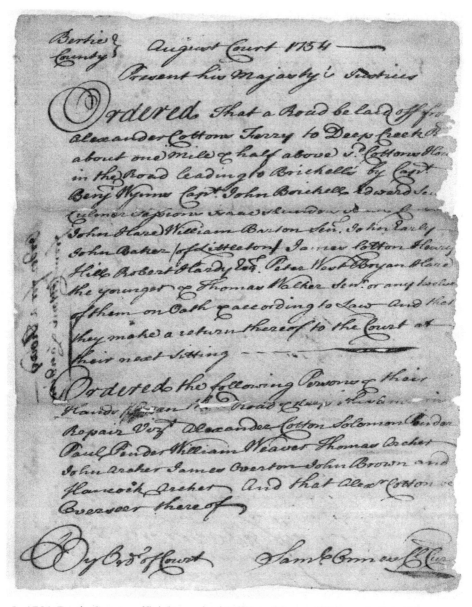

In 1754, Bertie County officials required William Weaver, Thomas Archer, John Archer, and Hancock Archer along with several of their white neighbors to work on the road from Alexander Cotton's Ferry to Deep Creek. (State Archives of North Carolina)

promised to teach apprentices to read and write, feed and lodge them, and provide them with freedom dues, which might include clothing or cash, at the end of their term of service.[11]

As well-integrated members of their community, free people of color regularly appeared in the local courts as plaintiffs and defendants in criminal and civil cases. Evidence from the eighteenth century demonstrates that during this time period, free persons of color could receive favorable outcomes in the local courts. In 1754 and 1760, North Carolina lawmakers prohibited "all Negroes and Mulattoes, bond or free" and "Indian servants and slaves" from testifying in court against whites. [12] This law undoubtedly created problems for free people of color who sought recourse against their white neighbors. Nevertheless, free people of color continued to bring cases against whites and sometimes received favorable judgments from the courts.

As previously noted, fires during the nineteenth century destroyed most of Hertford County's eighteenth-century court records. Yet a scattering of surviving records from Bertie County and the regional superior court provide us with some idea of the case types in which free people of color found themselves involved. Free persons of color appeared in the courts as both alleged victims of crimes and as criminal defendants. During 1758, Bertie County officials pursed fornication and adultery charges against Gabriel and Solomon Manley for living out of wedlock with Sarah Jones and Mary Ellis, respectively. In 1771, jurors brought charges against James Nickens for allegedly stealing "one mare of a bay colour" from Moore Carter.[13] On October 13, 1798, Armstrong Archer, "a man of colour," along with two of his white neighbors, John Cooper and Joshua Ward, came before the Hertford County justice and accused Peter Evans, a white man, of "feloniously stealing a Horse the Property of

---

[11] Walter Clark, ed., *The State Records of North Carolina,* vol. 25 (Goldsboro: Nash Brothers, 1906), 418-419.
[12] Clark, *State Records of North Carolina,* vol. 25, 283, 445.
[13] *King v. James Nickins*, Edenton District Records of the Superior Court, Box 25, 1771, SANC.

In 1798, Armstrong Archer filed a complaint against Peter Evans for stealing his horse. (State Archives of North Carolina)

Armstrong Archer."[14] Civil cases involving free people of color as plaintiffs against whites include Gabriel Manley's case against Barnaby Godwin during the late 1750s and James Nickens suit against Isaac Carter for a debt in the 1760s and 1770s. White people also brought civil charges against free people of color. In 1761, John Fennell sued Isaac Hall for nine pounds and eight pence. In the 1760s and 1770s, Matthias Brickell pursed a case against James Nickens for a debt.[15]

Free people of color sometimes won their cases against their white neighbors while in other instances their white neighbors came out of the courtroom victorious. Gabriel Manley's 1758 civil suit against Barnaby Godwin over an alleged assault ended with a favorable ruling from the court. The court took over a decade to award James Nickens a positive judgment in his case against local slaveholder Isaac Carter. Matthias Brickell's case against James Nickens during the late 1760s and early 1770s, however, landed Nickens in a less favorable situation. In 1773, the district court ruled against Nickens and required him to pay his debt to Brickell along with Brickell's court costs. Unable to pay the debt with cash, the court ordered the public sale of part of Nickens's corn crop. When the auction occurred, none of Nickens's neighbors made a bid for the corn, and the court gave the crop to Brickell as payment for the debt and court costs.[16]

With the break out of the American Revolution, North Carolinians of all persuasions found themselves placed on one side or the other of the conflict. Hertford County's free people of color were no exception, and several families sacrificed their young men for the independence cause. Caleb Archer, Evans Archer, Jesse Archer, James Bowser, William Brown, Henry Chavis, Gabriel Manley, Mark Manley, Moses Manley, Jr., Solomon Manley, Malachi Nickens, Carter Nickens, Edward Nickens, Abraham Shoecraft, James Smith, Edward Weaver, and John Weaver all

---

[14] *State v. Peter Evans*, Edenton District Records of the Superior Court, Box 45, 1798, SANC.

[15] *Matthias Brickell v. James Nickins*, Edenton District Superior Court Civil Action Papers, Box 75, 1773, SANC.

[16] *Matthias Brickell v. James Nickins*, Edenton District Superior Court Civil Action Papers, Box 75, 1773, SANC.

served either in Hertford County's militia regiment, a state regiment, or with the Continental Army. During the war, these men discovered a great deal about the fledgling United States as they marched through various colonies with their units. Evans Archer remembered that he enlisted at Portsmouth, Virginia in 1780 and served with the Continental Army for nearly two years. Malachi Nickens recalled being present at the Battle of Eutaw Springs in South Carolina and also participating in an engagement with Native peoples near the Savannah River.[17]

By the end of the American Revolution and dawn of the nineteenth century, free people of color had established a strong foothold in Hertford County's social, economic, and political life. They were landholders, workers, neighbors, and friends. Into the nineteenth century, free people of color would continue to maintain these positions. Yet the state's and nation's decisions to allow slavery to continue would lead to problems for free people of color in Hertford County and around the country. Slavery and the racial ideologies used to support the enslavement of hundreds of thousands and soon to be millions of people tainted Hertford County's social fabric. The free status of some of the county's persons of color provided them with many legal and social privileges such as personal property ownership and the right to trial by jury. Nevertheless, the debate over slavery's role in society placed those privileges in jeopardy. In the nineteenth century, some politicians would argue that all people of color should be beneath all white people both legally and socially while the

---

[17] The Third Division of the Militia Draughted in the Regiment of Hertford County, Military Collection, 5-20 [1778-1780] Drafts & Enlistments Hertford Co, SANC; Application of Evans Archer, File S41415, *Revolutionary War Pension and Bounty-Land Warrant Application Files,* National Archives Microfilm Publication; Application of William Brown, File R1349, *Revolutionary War Pension and Bounty-Land Warrant Application Files,* National Archives Microfilm Publication; Application of Malachi Nickens, File S41925, *Revolutionary War Pension and Bounty-Land Warrant Application Files,* National Archives Microfilm Publication; Edward Weaver, Treasurer and Comptroller's Papers, Box 23, Weaver, Edward, SANC; Military Warrant No. 113, Secretary of State Land Grant Office, Warrants, Plats, etc., Carter County TN 1-3: 01-02, Davidson County TN 1-139, SANC; Military Warrant No. 172, Secretary of State Land Grant Office, Warrants, Plats, etc., Tennessee County TN 55-357, SANC; Military Warrant No. 225, Secretary of State Land Grant Office, Warrants, Plats, etc., Davidson County TN 140-335, SANC.

most radical of them called for the removal or enslavement of free people of color.

# Chapter 2:
# The Pre-Civil War Nineteenth Century

The nineteenth century brought tremendous change to the lives of free people of color in Hertford County. During the nineteenth century, an overall strengthening of the national economy, technological innovations, and a growing population transformed life for all Americans including free people of color. Yet, at the same time, radical pro-slavery politicians, who would eventually push the nation into a civil war, targeted free people of color through discriminatory legislation. Nevertheless, all of these societal transformations failed to displace free people of color from the core of society. Even as some politicians attempted to depict them as outsiders who needed to be moved to remote colonies in the Caribbean and Africa, Hertford County's free people of color, like their contemporaries in other areas, continued to be essential to the inner- and outer-workings of their neighborhoods. As contributors to the local economy, they performed vital work as labors, artisans, and domestics. Free people of color were a significant part of Hertford County's social fabric. We cannot understand nineteenth-century Hertford County's family and kinship structures, social networks, legal institutions, and public ethos without understanding free people of color as part of the picture.

The surviving Hertford County records provide a complex and diverse picture of social relations among free people of color and their neighbors. Free people of color, whites, and enslaved people lived in the same neighborhoods. Family ties attached Hertford County residents into an intricate web of kinship that sometimes blurred the lines between the enslaved and free as well as the white and the non-white. Public functions such as religious meetings and court days regularly brought free people of color, whites, and enslaved people into shared spaces. White-only spaces and public discrimination existed in Hertford County, but they did not completely define social relations in the region.

The union between Willis and Sally Jones Weaver was one of two marriages between the children of William Weaver and the children of Nancy Jones. Willis and Sally had 10 children, many of whom became important leaders in education and politics. Several of their children were among the first students at Hampton Institute in Virginia. Their descendants include farmers, educators, lawyers, doctors, business people, and community leaders. (State Archives of North Carolina)

For most of Hertford County's free people of color, other people who shared their status were at the center of their social world. Kinship connections going back at least to the colonial period along with close proximity and common status as free people of color pushed the various families into a complex web of social and familial relations. By the mid-1800s, the descendants of the free families of color who lived in Hertford County during the 1700s were heavily interrelated; many of them built strong bonds through intermarriage between families. Three daughters of Jesse Weaver: Fanny, Phebe, and Nancy married three sons of Noah Cotton and Christian Wiggins: Wiley, John, and Micajah, respectively, creating a close connection between the families. William Weaver's children developed similar ties with the Hall and Jones families. His daughter Angeline married Harvey Hall, and his daughter Jane married Allen Hall. Harvey and Allen were the sons of Margaret "Peggy" Hall.

Additionally, Weaver's children Willis and Milly married the children of Nancy Jones, Sally Jones and William Jones, respectively.[18] Some free people of color strengthened family by marrying cousins. Jasper Keene, who was born in the 1830s, explained that he was "about second cousins" to his wife Eliza Ann Smith Keene and sister-in-law Sallie.[19]

Geographic proximity encouraged and contributed to the development of relationships among free people of color as they rarely isolated themselves from other free persons of color. Jacob Smith, William Brown, William Hall, and Willis Weaver, all free men of color, were among the neighbors of Obed Smith, a free man of color, in 1844. When Sally Ann Hall received a tract of land from her uncle Andrew Hall in 1851, most of her neighbors were other free people of color including William Hall, James Smith's heirs, and Elias Wyatt.[20]

Relationships between individual free people of color often dated back to their childhoods. Meredith Lee, who was born in the 1810s, recalled that he had known William Bizzell, who was about a decade his elder, "ever since we were boys." As adults, Lee and Bizzell worked together "hewing timbers for shipbuilding."[21] Starkey Pugh stated that he had a similar level of familiarity with Elizabeth "Betsey" Manley Newsome, who was his "near neighbor," and declared that he had known her "all my life" as they "were raised near." In adulthood, Pugh "held the light" at Newsome's wedding to her husband Dempsey.[22] Willis Manley, who was born in the 1820s, recalled knowing William Thomas Lewis from their youth. Manley explained that he and Lewis "were play-boys together," were "raised in the same neighborhood," and "lived in the same neighborhood all our lives." This close connection with Lewis placed

---

[18] Hertford County Will Book A, 65-66, 219-220, SANC.

[19] Jasper Keen Deposition July 24, 1903, Elvey Lewis Pension, Civil War Pensions, National Archives and Records Administration (from here NARA).

[20] Obed Smith Deed to J. A. Anderson, John Vann Papers, Box 1, Deeds, etc. #3, SANC; Andrew Hall to S. A. Hall Deed of Gift, Hertford County Deeds, Box 4, Hale-Hamilton, SANC.

[21] Meredith Lee Affidavit September 9, 1882, William Bizzell Pension, Civil War Pensions, NARA.

[22] Starkey Pugh Affidavit October 18, 1880, Dempsey Newsome Pension, Civil War Pensions, NARA.

In 1851, Andrew Hall transferred property to his niece Sally Ann Hall, the daughter of his sister Penny Hall. Several of Sally Ann's neighbors were other free people of color including William Hall, Elias Wyatt, and James Smith's heirs. (State Archives of North Carolina)

Manley at most of the key events in Lewis's life. Manley recalled that Lewis "was first married to Mary Pugh[,] old Starkey Pugh's daughter. I was at his wedding when he married Mary." He lived so close to the Lewis family that he could hear Mary's "lamentations" on her death bed.[23]

Weddings brought together the long-time friends and family of free people of color. Friends or family served as members of the wedding parties. Nancy Smothers Green assisted as a "waiter" at Enoch Luton and Martha Keene's wedding in 1850 or 1851.[24] Recalling the early-1860s wedding of Mary Francis Melton and Thomas Spiers, Armesia Jones Watford remembered, "I was at the marriage of Francis and Thomas. They were married by ceremony…My older sister…was an attendant at this marriage. I went just to see them married. Even then some of the colored people were married by ceremony, when they called themselves doing right."[25] Free people of color generally held their weddings in one of two places: their parents' home or the residence of the local magistrate. Jane Bizzell Collins, the aunt of the bride, recalled that the 1856 wedding of Levi Collins and Mary Sears, performed by Dr. Richard H. Shield, took place "at the residence of the bride's mother, Acree Sears."[26] According to Mary Brown Howard, her early-1860s marriage to John Lazarus Howard occurred at the home of Howell Jones, the justice of the peace who married them.[27] In rare instances, free people of color married at alternative locations. According to William B. Copeland and John Hall, Boone Nickens and Penny Cone married on the "porch" of Starkey S. Harrell's store in the late 1850s.[28] During the pre-Civil War nineteenth-

[23] Willis Manly Deposition November 11, 1902, William T. Lewis Pension, Civil War Pensions, NARA.

[24] Nancy Green Affidavit December 14, 1887, Enoch Luton Pension, Civil War Pensions, NARA.

[25] Armecy Watford Deposition April 9, 1924, James A. Lewis Pension, Civil War Pensions, NARA.

[26] Jane Collins Affidavit July 23, 1888, Jane Collins Affidavit December 12, 1888, Levi Collins Pension, Civil War Pensions, NARA.

[27] Mary Howard Deposition August 29, 1912, John Lazarus Howard Pension, Civil War Pensions, NARA.

[28] William B. Copeland Deposition November 18, 1910, Boone Nickens Pension, Civil War Pensions, NARA; John Hall Deposition November 21, 1910, Boone Nickens Pension, Civil War Pensions, NARA.

Sallie Matilda Smith's first marriage was to Edward Weaver. With the support of Betsey Smith, her stepmother, and Becky Davis, Sallie gave birth to the couple's first and only child, Homozilla Weaver. After Edward Weaver's death during the Civil War, Sallie married Elvey D. Lewis. (Private Collection)

century, local magistrates not ministers married most free people of color. William Bizzell and Elizabeth Wyatt Bizzell recalled that when they attended the 1830s wedding of Nathaniel Wyatt and Martha "Patsey" Weaver, James Wynn, the "acting justice of the peace," officiated at the ceremony.[29] Jane Archer Flood, discussing her late-1840s wedding, explained, "I married Bolden Flood when I was 13 or 14 years old. Pell Sessoms a magistrate a white man married us…at a place called Long Branch."[30]

Furthermore, the births of children in the community strengthened the bonds among free women of color. They assisted and comforted one another during their children's deliveries. Nancy Manley Pugh, a midwife, recollected being with Elizabeth Manley Newsome "during her confinements," which would have taken place between the 1840s and 1860s.[31] Betsey Smith and Becky Davis attended the birth of Homozilla

[29] William Bissell and Elizabeth Bissell Deposition March 6, 1876, Richard Wyatt Pension, Civil War Pensions, NARA.
[30] Jane Flood Deposition May 15, 1899, Bolden Flood Pension, Civil War Pensions, NARA.
[31] Nancy Pugh Deposition August 14, 1893, Dempsey Newsome Pension, Civil War Pensions, NARA.

Weaver, daughter of Sallie Matilda Smith Weaver and Edward Weaver in 1861.[32] The free women of color who attended births provided mothers with their expert experience during these exciting, yet dangerous events. During the nineteenth century, childbirth was one of the leading causes of death for women, and attendants played an imperative role in protecting the lives of mothers and babies.

In addition to aiding with the births of children, free people of color often assisted one another during family struggles. After the passing of parents, free people of color took in the orphans of family and friends. Following their parents' deaths in the mid-1810s, the orphans of Noah Cotton and Christian Wiggins lived with other free people of color in their neighborhood. At various times, David, James, and Jemima Weaver cared for the couples' daughter Lucinda Cotton. Enos Stafford lodged their son William Cotton at his home while Solomon and Phereby Keene housed, fed, clothed, and educated Richard and John Cotton. Free people of color also supported their neighbors in financial need. Stephen and John Archer recalled assisting their kinsmen Levi Archer, a disabled person, and his family during hard times.[33] Tryal Williamson provided support to Charles Weaver's family during financial troubles. Williamson's son Eli recalled "that Charles Weaver was a man of feeble constitution—that in the year 1841 my father Tryal Williamson hired the said Charles to work upon the farm during that year for wages less than a good farm hand was worth— that from ill health he would have been discharged had it not been for sympathy for his needy and suffering family."[34]

Like many other North Carolinians, some free people of color left their home state for opportunities in the west, and when they made their treks to the west they often travelled with their extended families and close friends. The first major exodus from Hertford County took place during

---

[32] Becky Davis and Betsey Smith Deposition December 6, 1866, Edward Weaver Pension, Civil War Pensions, NARA.

[33] John Vann Papers, Box 3, Estate Noah Cotton 1815, SANC; Stephen Archer and John Archer Deposition November 15, 1882, George Archer Pension, Civil War Pensions, NARA.

[34] Eli Williamson Deposition July 3, 1883, Richard R. Weaver Pension, Civil War Pensions, NARA.

Jeremiah Stafford was one of many free people of color to leave Hertford County to settle in the Midwest during the first half of the nineteenth century. After leaving North Carolina, Stafford and his family moved to Indiana before settling in Michigan. (Private Collection)

the first decades of the nineteenth century. Members of the Archer and Nickens families left the area and settled in Tennessee. A much larger migration of families to different parts of Ohio, Indiana, and Michigan took place after this initial removal. Portions of the Bizzell, Bowser, Brown, Cotton, Garnes, Hall, Lee, Melton, Robbins, Shoecraft, Stafford, Weaver, Wiggins, and Wyatt families left Hertford County and resettled in these areas. Families such as the Shoecrafts and Meltons took over a generation to finally make their way to the Midwest. These families stopped in Orange and Guilford Counties in North Carolina before finally settling in Indiana. As a result of these migrations, several family names disappeared among Hertford County's free people of color including Shoecraft, Stafford, and Wyatt.[35]

Ahead of their westward treks, free people of color requested papers from local officials proving their free status. Prior to leaving Hertford County, Nathaniel Wyatt and Martha "Patsey" Weaver Wyatt obtained a document that certified their family's freedom. Their papers, signed by the county's justices of the peace in 1844, explained, "This will certify that Nathan Wyat[t] a free man of color was free born and born of free parents he is about forty years of age five feet ten Inches high of dark copper complexion with a scar on the Right side of his face & six fingers on his left hand." The justices also attested that "he is of Industrious habbits [sic] and of good c[h]aracter." The free papers further revealed "that Patsy Wyat[t] his wife was free born and born of free parents she is about thirty Eight years of age of a light yellow complexion with straight black hare." Additionally, the statement described "that Penna Wyat[t] is the daughter of said Patsey & Nathan Wyat[t] she is about fourteen years of age of a yellow complexion Also the Iry Wyat[t] is the son of said Patsey & Nathan Wyat[t] he is about Eleven years of age of a dark copper complexion." The papers only explained that "Henry a boy about nine years of age and Armecy about six years of age are the children of said

---

[35] Sumner County Will Book, 1789-1842, 122, Tennessee Wills and Probate Records; National Archives Microfilm Publication, *Eastern Cherokee Applications of the U.S. Court of Claims, 1906-1909*, M1104; John Weaver Affidavit May 5, 1879, Sarah Wyatt Affidavit April 11, 1891, Richard Wyatt Pension, Civil War Pensions, NARA; Abner Bizzell Deposition January 24, 1884, Abner Bizzell Pension, Civil War Pensions, NARA.

Patsy & Nathan Wyat[t]."[36] Winborn Garnes took similar actions as the Wyatts before relocating to Ohio. His papers simply explained, "Winborn Garnes a free man of colour was born and raised in this county of free parents aged about twenty three years about six feet high of tolerable light complexion with a small scar near the right eye and has always born a good character."[37] Documents such as these were important protection against people who might try to question or obscure their free status.

The movements of Hertford County's free people of color were not limited to long-distance journeys to the west. At least since the mid-1700s, free people of color had participated in wide social networks that connected them with relatives and associates in neighboring counties and other parts of the region. Up until the middle of the nineteenth-century, free people of color in Hertford County maintained close relations with family and friends in Norfolk and Princess Anne counties in Virginia; some actually lived in both locations. Willis Bass, Abner and Martin Bizzell, Evans and Mathuel Archer, William and Levi Collins, and William Shoecraft are a few of the individuals who lived in both Hertford County and the Virginia communities.[38]

Other free persons of color kept strong connections with people in neighboring counties such as Pasquotank, Perquimans, Gates,

---

[36] Wyatt Family Free Papers, Richard Wyatt Pension, Civil War Pensions, NARA.
[37] Register of Blacks in Ohio Counties, 1804-1861, Ross County, 1804-1855, 146, Ohio History Center.
[38] William Bass to Willis Bass, Norfolk County Deed Book 45, 1, LVA; Abner Bizzle to Miss Elizabeth Gibbs Marriage Bond, Norfolk County Marriage Bonds, 1811, LVA; Martin Biswell to Elizabeth Seirs Marriage Bond, Norfolk County Marriage Bonds, 1817-1820, LVA; Norfolk County Tithables 1774 Unidentified District Enumerated by David Porter, Norfolk County Tithable Lists, 1752-1783, LVA; Petition of Eli & Wm Copeland of Hertford County, General Assembly Session Records, November-December 1807, Box 2, (Nov.-Dec., 1807) Joint Committee Reports (Propositions and Grievances), SANC; Application of Evans Archer, File S41415, *Revolutionary War Pension and Bounty-Land Warrant Application Files,* National Archives Microfilm Publication; *Muster Rolls of the Soldiers of the War of 1812: Detached from the Militia of North Carolina, In 1812 and 1814* (Raleigh: CH. C. Raboteau, 1851), 7-8; 1818 Tax List, Auditor of Public Accounts Personal Property Tax Books, Norfolk County, 1813-1824, 1, 3, LVA; 1860 U. S. Federal Census, Hertford County, North Carolina; 1850 U. S. Federal Census, Hertford County, North Carolina; William Shewcraft and Selah to Kinner Collins, Princess Anne County Deed Book 23, 226, LVA.

In 1820, Polly Gibbs Mitchell received free papers from a Hertford County justice of the peace. The document certified Polly's status as a free person and provided important information about her family background. (State Archives of North Carolina)

Northampton, and Bertie in North Carolina. Intermarriages between free people of color from these counties and Hertford County occurred regularly. Migrations of people from these counties to Hertford County or from Hertford County to these counties were quite common. Pennina Boone who moved from Gates County to Hertford County recalled, "I was born in Gates Co. but was raised by my uncle Tom Rob[b]ins of Winton N. C. I am the daughter of Abram Boone but I was left an orphan so my uncle raised me."[39] Similar to those people who moved outside of the state, those free people of color who moved within North Carolina requested papers to document their status as free persons. In 1820, Polly Gibbs Mitchell, who left Hertford County for Pasquotank County, received papers certifying her free status. Under oath, Polly's aunt Phereby Keene swore that "Polly Mitchell wife of Allen Mitchell—was formerly Polly Gibbs…that she was born free and always remained free that she…was the daughter of Lucy Gibbs who was sister to her." In support of Keene's statement, John Copeland affirmed that Polly's mother Lucy Gibbs "was born free and was always considered to be a free person."[40] These statements were of particular importance because North Carolina law granted freedom to an individual based on the freedom status of that individual's mother, regardless of racial classification.

Since the colonial period, free persons of color and white people lived in fairly close proximity to one another. As neighbors and friends, white Hertford County residents paid attention to the happenings and affairs of local free persons of color. Thomas O'Dwyer, an Irish physician based in Murfreesboro who lived near free people of color, recorded their activities. For example, O'Dwyer noted in his writings when his neighbors of color were sick or died. On April 9, 1825, O'Dwyer wrote of the passing of 45-year-old Nathan Boone, a "mul[att]o," and explained that Boone had suffered from rheumatism for years and also dealt with convulsive fits. On the eighteenth of that same month, he also wrote, "Heard Nancy Tann a

---

[39] Pennina Reynolds Deposition November 21, 1902, Hampton Reynolds Pension, Civil War Pensions, NARA.
[40] Polly Mitchell Free Papers, Perquimans County Slave Records, Box 2, Certificates of Free Negroes, No date, 1733-1861, SANC.

mul[att]o girl, about 18 y[ea]rs old died this afternoon—she was sister to Harrison."[41] For O'Dwyer, the free people of color in his community were not anonymous others but neighbors with histories connected to his own.

White people and free people of color sometimes relied on one another during times of need. After a fire broke out at one of his properties, William D. Valentine, a white man, found himself in debt to Nathaniel "Nat" Turner, a free man of color. On a November morning in 1854, following breakfast, a fire began to consume a home owned by Valentine and occupied by A. G. Brett. Someone discovered that the building's "shingles were smoking," and a woman cried out for help. Valentine heard the noise, but Turner came to the rescue. Turner climbed to the top of the building and received buckets of water from below. With the assistance of Valentine and the others on the ground, Turner put out the fire. At the conclusion of the event, Valentine praised Turner for performing "good service, grateful service."[42]

Geographic closeness encouraged the development of intimate relationships between free people of color and whites in Hertford County. Some free people of color and whites participated in casual sexual relations or concubinage. In 1853, William D. Valentine, discussing the presence of a large population of "free persons of color" around Winton, observed, "This class, mulattoes, are much under the influences of the whites. There is a deal of impurity with the females of the low degraded race. Degrading practices of this kind have long no doubt been common here and formerly to a greater extent than now. But they are too bad now. Colored girls of which there are yet many are a fearful bane to the morals of young white men. So common has it long been that I apprehend it is too much tolerated by married men in this locality. They too indulge. The whites are more blamable than the low degraded colored. These consider it no disgrace."[43]

---

[41] Thomas O'Dwyer Diary, Samuel Jordan Wheeler Diaries, Volume 1, SHC.
[42] William D. Valentine Diary, Volume 14, 110, SHC.
[43] William D. Valentine Diary, Volume 13, 85, SHC.

Mollie Cherry Hall was the daughter of Sally Ann Hall and Albert G. Vann. Her mother was her father's concubine. Speaking of her father as an adult, Mollie declared, "I despised my white father and his folks. I might have loved him if he had noticed and treated us like other folks." After leaving home, she married the successful politician, educator, and leader Joseph B. Catus. (Private Collection)

The testimony of Mollie Cherry Hall, the daughter of Sally Ann Hall, a free woman of color, and Albert G. Vann, a white man, provides insight into one of these intimate relationships. She recalled the life of her mother, Vann's mistress, and her family. Mollie, who was born in the 1850s, stated, "I despised my white father and his folks. I might have loved him if he had noticed and treated us like other folks. His wife died after a while but she never fussed as I know of about his colored family. He had large children, some grown. He did not stay at home. He would have the work done by Negro slaves." Mollie further recollected that Vann "would eat at my mother's house. She called him 'the man,' and we called him 'the man.' He would come in at bed-time and even before his wife died he would come and stay with my mother all night and get up and go to his house the next morning." Concluding her discussion of her parents' relationship and her childhood, Mollie explained, "His children despised us and I despised them and all their folks, and I despised him. We had to work hard, get no education, and but a little to live on. He had plenty of property but didn't give mother one thing. Her uncle gave her her home and field. We had to work it."[44]

Other free people of color and whites developed serious long-term relationships, which in many ways were like marriage, except for legal recognition. Although North Carolina at first discouraged and later outright banned marriage between free people of color and whites, the law and some level of social discouragement could not completely prevent the development of familial relations between them. During the late 1700s and early nineteenth century, Noah Cotton, a white man, and Christian "Kiddy" Wiggins, a free woman of color, engaged in a marriage-like relationship. The union between Noah and Christian produced at least nine children, whom the couple raised together. At least some people in their neighborhood accepted their relationship as legitimate and referred to Christian and her children by the Cotton surname, implying the validity of the relationship. In 1812, Noah Cotton dictated a will leaving his plantation and lands to the couple's sons and the rest of his property to the sons, their sisters, and Christian. In the 1815 codicil to the 1812 will, Noah unambiguously acknowledged his sons and daughters with Christian as "my children."[45] By the mid-1840s, Celia Garnes, a free woman of color, and Wiley Ezell, a white, had begun to build their relationship on an equally strong foundation. Garnes and Ezell lived in the same house and raised their children together. In order to secure his rights to his children, Ezell had the court bind his sons with Garnes to him as apprentices. This arrangement assured that the children would remain in their parents' custody and work for their family's benefit. Familial relationships between free people of color and whites also included families headed by free men of color and white women. From the 1830s through the 1860s, Henry

---

[44] "Catus Family History," E. Franklin Frazier Papers Box 131–92, Folder 7; Manuscript Division, Moorland-
Spingarn Research Center, Howard University. Mollie Cherry Hall married Joseph B. Catus. Her statement about her mother receiving land from her uncle is confirmed by a deed. The deed from Andrew Hall to his niece Sally Ann Hall also mentions Sally's mother Penny Hall, Andrew's sister. See Andrew Hall to S. A. Hall Deed of Gift, Hertford County Deeds, Box 4, Hale-Hamilton, SANC.
[45] Estate of Christian Cotton, John Vann Papers, Box 3, Estate Cotten, Christian 1816, SANC; Will of Noah Cotton, John Vann Papers, Box 4, Will Noah Cotton 1815, SANC.

Best, a free man of color, and Elizabeth Baker, a white woman, shared a home and had several children. Although the law failed to recognize their union, David Boone, a free man of color, and Louvenia Britt, a white woman, also lived together and raised their son Richard Britt from at least the 1840s to the 1860s.[46]

During the nineteenth century, Hertford County's free people of color and whites performed civic duties together. Until a state constitutional convention disenfranchised them in 1835, free men of color voted alongside whites in elections. One source suggests that there may have been as many as 150 free men of color voting in Hertford County at the time. In addition, several free people of color served in a local regiment at the beginning of the War of 1812. Josiah Robbins, John Bizzell, John Weaver, Mathuel Archer, Ephraim King, Samuel Boone, Elijah Archer, and William Brown were members of the regiment. Most of these men who served with their neighbors would not finish the war as soldiers. In 1812, the North Carolina legislature prohibited free men of color from serving with the militia as troops. Silas Shoecraft was the only free person of color allowed to remain with the Hertford County service men until war's end, but only as a fifer.[47] Furthermore, as in the colonial period, free people of color worked along with whites on county road projects. In 1853, the county court ordered Thomas Robbins, Jr, Arthur Reynolds, Joseph Hall, Washington Lang, Boone Nickens, William Nickens, Manuel Reynolds, Smith Green, and Thomas Reynolds to labor beside 12 of their white neighbors "or their hands" to restore local roads.[48]

Free people of color also obtained their educations along with white people or with the assistance of white people before the Civil War although a 1840s state law prohibited free people of color from attending public schools for whites. Rufus H. Reynolds, who was a small child before the end of the Civil War, recalled that free people of color went to school with whites during the period. White people also aided in the

---

[46] Hertford County Court Minutes, Volume 2, 126, 156, 178, SANC.
[47] *Proceedings and Debates of the Convention of North-Carolina, Called to Amend the Constitution of the State; Which Assembled at Raleigh, June 4, 1835* (Raleigh: Joseph Gales and Son, 1836), 80; *Muster Rolls of the Soldiers of the War of 1812*, 7-8, 76.
[48] Hertford County Court Minutes, Volume 3, 545, SANC.

instruction of children of color before the war. For instance, after the deaths of Noah Cotton and Christian Wiggins in the mid-1810s, James McPherson, a white teacher, tutored the couples' children.[49]

Churches were another important community space in which free people of color regularly cooperated with whites and enslaved people. During most of the pre-Civil War period, free people of color attended churches with mixed congregations exclusively. The surviving records for Mount Tabor Baptist Church list John and Sarah Bizzell along with Ann and Mary Reynolds as members of the congregation. Through the Civil War, members of the Reynolds, Melton, Weaver, Nickens, Jones, Bowens, Haithcock, Smith, Shepherd, Boone, Britt, and Turner families were among the worshipers at the Meherrin Baptist Church.[50] Before North Carolina lawmakers prohibited them from preaching during the General Assembly's 1831-1832 session, free men of color worked as ministers in Hertford County. In 1804, Jacob Archer received a license to preach from the Baptist church.[51] Immediately before the enactment of the preaching ban, London Gee also served as a Baptist minister.[52] After the preaching ban, free people of color participated in congregations as members with limited privileges. White men held most positions of power within the churches. The white leaders in the Meherrin Baptist Church, however, allowed free people of color and slaves some control over members of their own status.[53] In addition, free people of color also assisted in church maintenance. During 1852, Mount Tabor Baptist Church paid four dollars to Jesse Reynolds "for repairs done by him to the meetinghouse well."[54] Furthermore, white church leaders included free people of color in church charity efforts. On several occasions, the Meherrin Baptist Church dedicated funds to the upkeep of Dempsey Weaver. The church helped to

---

[49] *The Ahoskie Era of Hertford County* (Ahoskie: Parker Brothers, 1939), 252; John Vann Papers, Box 3, Estate Noah Cotton 1815, SANC.

[50] Mt. Tabor Baptist Church Minutes and Various Records, SANC; Meherrin Baptist Church Minutes, 106, 121, 131, 132, 146-147, 152, 173, 184-186, 231, SANC.

[51] Enoch Hutchinson, editor, *The Baptist Memorial and Monthly Record, Volume 6* (New York: E. Hutchinson, 1848), 368.

[52] Solon Borland to Roscius C. Borland, Governors Papers, Volume 62, SANC.

[53] Meherrin Baptist Church Minutes, 149, 212, SANC.

[54] Mt. Tabor Baptist Church Minutes and Various Records, September 1852, SANC.

In 1850, several free people of color decided to leave the white-dominated churches and establish Pleasant Plains Baptist Church. The next year, the church was admitted to the Chowan Baptist Association as the organization's first church for free persons of color. After the Civil War, the church joined other congregations of color in the Roanoke Missionary Baptist Association. From its founding into the twenty-first century, Pleasant Plains played an important role in the social and religious lives of Hertford County's free people of color and their descendants. (Private Collection)

provide for his basic needs during his sickness, and upon the death of this free man of color, the church family paid his funeral expenses.[55]

    Some free people of color sought more autonomy from whites and helped to establish Pleasant Plains Baptist Church in the 1850s. Thomas Hoggard, a white preacher, served as the church's minister and Hoggard along with Henry Modlin and Joseph A. Mizzell, both white men, represented the church during meetings of the Chowan Baptist Association, the regional Baptist organization. Yet the establishment of Pleasant Plains allowed free people of color a greater level of control over the direction of their congregation than they enjoyed in the county's other religious centers. On August 30, 1850, Jesse Keene, William Jones, Arthur Reynolds, Jacob Smith, Simon Bizzell, William Hall, Nathaniel "Nat"

---

[55] Meherrin Baptist Church Minutes, 186, 202, SANC.

Turner, John Bizzell, and Willis Weaver contracted with Lawrence Weaver to construct the church building. In 1852, 57 free people of color had joined the Pleasant Plains congregation. By 1860, the congregation included 219 members. No white people or enslaved people were members of the congregation. Free people of color left the surrounding churches in mass in order to become part of the new fellowship.[56]

Although only free people of color were among Pleasant Plains Baptist Church's congregants, whites occasionally participated in the church's events. On October 15, 1855, William D. Valentine along with a few other white people attended the baptisms of 26 free people of color in the Chowan River at Barfields. All of those who the minister baptized became parishioners at Pleasant Plains. Valentine commented that the "colored church now in existence some half dozen years seems productive of much good. This class of people between the negro and the white, without the protection of the one and the privileges of the other, is much ameliorated in a moral and religious state in this neighborhood."[57]

With enslaved people making up a significant portion of Hertford County's pre-Civil War population, free people of color encountered them in daily life beyond church. Yet the surviving historical records suggest that familial relationships between free people of color and enslaved people were uncommon. Different family origins coupled with unequal legal, political, and economic statuses as well as disparities in educational attainment likely created fissures in general relations between the majority of free people of color and most of the enslaved population. A significant number of Hertford County's free people of color descended from the families who had been free during the eighteenth century. Therefore, their genealogies left many with few to no ancestral or familial ties to slaves. The surviving historical records reveal more domestic and intimate relationships among free people of color and those between free people of

---

[56] *Genealogy of the Collins-Bizzell Families, Third Publication* (Washington: Paul E. Sluby, Sr. and William K. Collins, Sr., 1988), 179-180; *Minutes of the Chowan Baptist Association* (Raleigh: Biblical Recorder Office, 1852), 8-9; *Minutes of the Fifty Fourth Annual Session of the Chowan Baptist Association Held with the Church at Edenton, NC* (1860), 12-13.

[57] William D. Valentine Diary, Volume 15, 72-73, SHC.

color and whites than partnerships between free persons of color and slaves. Bryant Manley who grew up during the antebellum period was the son of Parthena Manley, a free woman of color, and Abram Barnes, an enslaved man, but people like Bryant Manley appear to have been more of a rarity than the norm.[58]

Slaveholding by free people of color was equally rare but still a noteworthy feature of some relationships between enslaved people and free persons of color. At the estate sale of James Crawford on 31 April 1814, Willis Nickens purchased an enslaved girl named Rose. The 1830 census lists a small number of free persons of color with slaves in their households including David Boone, Penelope Manley, Meady Melton, Jeston Reynolds, and David Roberts. By 1850, however, slaves rarely appeared in the households of free people of color in Hertford County. Jarvis Reynolds was the only free person of color to appear in that year's census slave schedule with a slave in his household. Reynolds kept one woman in her seventies. The nature of the master-slave relationship is unclear.[59]

Free people of color and slaves, however, had an assortment of relationships beyond the familial or master-slave interaction. Some free people of color employed slaves to work under them. Peggy Weaver hired the slaves of her white Murfreesboro neighbor Thomas O'Dwyer. On multiple occasions, Bob and Peter, two men owned by O'Dwyer worked for Weaver.[60] Free people of color and enslaved people also labored side by side. Baccus Holly, who was enslaved, recalled working along with Alfred Bailey, a free person of color, in their youthful days. In a statement, Holly explained that Bailey "and his boss man were hired by my old master and we used to work together at the fish nets. We fished hard and I

---

[58] Bryant Manley Deposition September 3, 1902, Bryant Manley Pension, Civil War Pensions, NARA.

[59] Account of the Sales of the Perishable Estate of James Crafford, John Vann Papers, Box 3, Estate- Crawford, James 1814, SANC; 1830 U. S. Federal Census, Hertford County, North Carolina; 1850 U. S. Federal Census Slave Schedules, Southern District, Hertford County, North Carolina.

[60] Thomas O'Dwyer Diary, August 19, December 13, 1825, SHC.

remember that he worked with us in the rain and did good work."[61] Free people of color and enslaved people were also neighbors. Dorsey Shaw, who was enslaved before the Civil War, stated that he had known Jane Flood, a free woman of color, "since she was a child." Jane's mother Polly Archer "lived about one and half miles" from William Shaw, Dorsey's master, and Dorsey saw the Archers "often" and "knew them intimately."[62]

During the first decade of the nineteenth century, a group of free men of color along with some of their white neighbors assisted an enslaved man from their community in seeking his liberty. In 1807, Eli and William Copeland petitioned the North Carolina General Assembly for the right to emancipate Ben, who was "in their possession as a slave." They contended "that it is incompatible with the tenets of Christianity which they profess to hold any of the human race in servile Bondage." In support of the Copelands' request, the following free men of color signed an adjoining petition: Abner Bizzell, James Smith, William Smith, Edward Weaver, Willis Nickens, William Brown, Dempsey Reid, Jeremiah Reid, and Daniel Garnes. These free men of color and some of their white neighbors declared they were "willing that...Ben be a free man among us as he is under good carrecter [character] in our county and in other places whear [where] he is known."[63] Although Ben held a different legal status, for these free men, he was a noteworthy and integral part of the neighborhood.

Some free people of color likely sympathized with the plight of enslaved people because of the effects slavery's existence had on their lives. Unscrupulous characters involved in the domestic slave trade were a widespread threat to free people of color in Hertford County and across the country. These individuals sought profits by illegally kidnapping free people of color and selling them outside of their home communities as

---

[61] Baccus Holly Deposition July 30, 1895, Alfred Bailey Pension, Civil War Pensions, NARA.

[62] Dorsey Shaw Affidavit December 15, 1897, Bolden Flood Pension, Civil War Pensions, NARA.

[63] Petition of Eli & Wm Copeland of Hertford County, General Assembly Session Records, November-December 1807, Box 2, (Nov.-Dec., 1807) Joint Committee Reports (Propositions and Grievances), SANC.

## KIDNAPPING.

ON or about the 29th of December last, a certain THOMAS WIGGINS, a small impudent looking fellow, about 35 or 40 years old, endowed with an extraordinary *gift of the gab*, departed hence for the upper Counties, with three Horses and a Waggon loaded with Brandy, intended for sale ; and took with him as an assistant, JESSE MAND-LY, a free lad of color, spare made, 17 or 18 years old, curly hair, sharp forehead and fierce looking eyes ; his clothes I am unable to describe. Wiggins has but lately return-ed, without the Boy, and says that he was killed by the tongue of the waggon. There are strong circumstances to induce a belief, that he has sold him for a Slave ; indeed, I entertain not the smallest doubt of it.

He who will behold a fellow-citizen de-prived of his liberty, without giving aid to rescue him, is unworthy the enjoyment of it himself. It is therefore, that I offer a reward of ONE HUNDRED DOLLARS for such information as will enable me to punish the guilty WIGGINS, and relieve the innocent and suffering Mandly.

JOS. F. DICKINSON.
Winton, Hertford county, N. C.
April 5                                     69 3w

☞ Printers in South-Carolina, Georgia, Tennessee and Kentucky, who know the va-lue of freedom, will give this advertisement two or three insertions in their respective papers.                              J. F. D.

After Thomas Wiggins, a white man, returned to Hertford County without Jesse Manley, a free boy of color, Joseph F. Dickinson placed an advertisement in local newspapers, which requested the boy's return. Dickinson suspected Wiggins had kidnapped Manley and sold him into slavery. The advertisement appeared in the April 17, 1818 edition of Raleigh's *Weekly Register*. (Newspapers.com)

slaves. At least one free person of color from Hertford County became a victim of one of these illicit dealers. In 1818, Joseph F. Dickenson reported the kidnapping of Jesse Manley. He described Manley as "a free lad of color, spare made, 17 or 18 years old, curly hair, sharp forehead and fierce looking eyes." Dickenson explained that Thomas Wiggins, "a small impudent looking fellow, about 35 or 40 years old, endowed with an extraordinary gift of the gab" left with Manley in his assistance on an alleged trip to sell a wagon load of brandy but "returned, without the Boy, and says that he was killed by the tongue of the waggon [sic]." Unconvinced by Wiggins's story of Manley's demise, Dickenson relayed to newspaper subscribers, "There are strong circumstances to induce a belief, that he had sold him for a Slave; indeed, I entertain not the smallest doubt of it." In the conclusion of his advertisement, Dickenson declared, "He who will behold a fellow-citizen deprived of his liberty, without giving aid to rescue him, is unworthy the enjoyment of it himself."[64]

Although whites and enslaved people made up a greater portion of Hertford County's population than free people of color, this segment of the population still had vital role in the local economy. Free people of color contributed to the community by providing labor and services to their neighbors; some were common laborers while others had more skilled occupations. Along with their work, free people of color participated in the economy as consumers. Both whites and other free people of color depended on them to support their business and supplement their incomes.

Living in a community heavily centered on agriculture, free people of color worked the fields and operated their own farms. They raised a variety of different animals and cultivated various types of produce. Benjamin Archer kept hogs and grew greens, corn, potatoes, and apples on his farm. The more prosperous free people of color owned farms and hired laborers to work them. Both Eli Williamson and his father Tryal Williamson before him employed laborers to work their farms. Other free people of color rented land. In 1832, Allen Hall leased a plantation from the heirs of Jesse Vann. Men, women, and children all participated in farm

---

[64] "Kidnapping," *Weekly Raleigh Register*, 17 April 1818.

As a girl, Sarah Eliza Weaver, along with her siblings, labored on Eli
Williamson's farm in order to support her family. The Weaver family
depended on the labor of their children because Charles Weaver, Sarah Eliza's
father, was sickly and unable to work. (Private Collection)

work. After the death of his father David in the 1859, the teenage John Cumbo traveled from place to place laboring on the farms of his neighbors in order to support his mother Nancy. [65] John Thomas Weaver, who was born in the early 1840s, remembered that during his younger days, he "did nothing but farm work."[66]

Free people of color played an essential part in the local fishing economy, providing both labor and years of experience. Many free people of color worked in the regional fishing industry as suppliers for major fisheries and merchants. Merchants depended on fishermen to catch the fish and women to process the catch. In turn, fishermen and cleaners relied on local merchants to purchase their products and services. John Bizzell and Simon Bizzell were among the many free men of color who fished the local waters. Local businessmen like John Vann regularly purchased large catches of herring and shad from the Bizzells and other free men of color, which he may have used on his own plantation or sold on the market.[67]

North Carolina merchant John B. Chesson relied on both enslaved and free laborers to work in his fishing operation on the North Carolina coast. To satisfy labor requirements, Chesson called on white Hertford County businessman John A. Anderson to recruit laborers from Anderson's home county and send those laborers by boat to Washington County to work. In 1849, Anderson hired Jesse Reynolds and Benjamin Weaver as hands, and Velia Bizzell, Sally Butler, Barsha Reynolds, and Feraby Melton to work as fish cutters. He also rented several enslaved men, all described as "molatto," to labor as hands. In a letter to Chesson, Anderson complained that he had a very difficult time finding women workers, and expressed fear that he would lose Sally Butler to someone offering her a better opportunity. Despite a high demand for and a scarcity of women familiar with cleaning fish, male hands made nearly twice as much as female

---

[65] Hertford County Record of Estates, Volume 3, 396-397; Eli Williamson Deposition December 29, 1884, Richard R. Weaver Pension, Civil War Pensions, NARA; Hertford County Guardian Accounts, Volume 1, 107, SANC; James Turner and John Turner Deposition November 13, 1873, John Cumbo Pension, Civil War Pensions, NARA.
[66] John T. Weaver Deposition February 3, 1897, John T. Weaver Pension, Civil War Pensions, NARA.
[67] John Vann Papers, Box 2, Fishery Accounts 1828-1832, SANC.

The family of Wiley and Mary Wyatt Jones produced numerous success stories in business, civic work, and education. Before the Civil War, Wiley Jones worked as a brick mason and farmed. Pictured in the front row are Wiley Jones, Mary Wyatt Jones, Nancy Jones Turner, Armesia Jones Turner Watford, and Susan Jones Melton. Standing in the back row are Albert Jones, Texanna Jones Jenkins, Warren "Sonny Boy" Jones, Delilah Jones Brown, Mary Elizabeth Jones Nickens, and Eff Richard Jones. (Private Collection)

cutters. Gender-based notions about work directly influenced wages, and employers paid men more than women. Even if white businessmen did not practice wage discrimination against individuals based on the racial designation, they practiced wage discrimination based on gender. Women like Velia Bizzell and Sally Butler, who were the heads of their own households, faced the same demands as men to support themselves and their families, but even men such as Benjamin Weaver, whom Anderson described as a "slow" worker, received better pay for a day's work.[68]

The Hertford County census records reveal that several free people of color made a living as skilled artisans. Free men of color worked as coopers, blacksmiths, carpenters, shoemakers, painters, and sawyers. In

---

[68] John B. Chesson Papers, Box 1, Miscellaneous, SANC.

particular, many affluent whites required the services of these tradesmen to keep their personal affairs, plantations, shipping operations, and merchant shops in working order. During the 1830s, Tryal Williamson and David Weaver crafted shoes for numerous white neighbors. Thomas Boone served the community as a blacksmith. Coopers like William Hall, Smith Green, and William David Newsome constructed the barrels that stored agricultural goods produced on local farms for shipment by boat. Bricks made by Wiley Jones and Jesse Keene were critical for many different construction jobs. Shop joiners such as Enoch Luton built windows and crafted doorways for homes and businesses. Painters Andrew and Benjamin Reynolds were essential for both new construction projects and the maintenance of older structures. William Dunston, who came to Hertford County from Franklin County, constructed mattresses.[69] Regardless of the success of some free people of color, whites, who held the majority of the county's wealth, had to be the key consumers of the skills and products of free people of color. These tradesmen of color had a clear understanding of their consumers, and skillfully and carefully worked to gain their business and trust. Real property ownership by many of the tradesmen suggests that they were successful entrepreneurs, and used the rewards of their work to build personal wealth that in some cases exceeded the holdings of many of their white and non-white neighbors.[70]

During the nineteenth century, Hertford County's apprenticeship system continued to influence the lives of free people of color. As in the colonial period, the courts regularly bound out free children of color to trades related to agriculture. In 1847, the county court sent Rachel Manley's son James to Lemuel R. Jernigan to be instructed in "Farming." At the next court session in May, officials bound Rebecca Weaver's son 6-year-old Jacob Davis to learn the same task under Lewis Snipes. Officials included free girls of color among those eligible to learn to farm. During the February 1845 session, they placed "Rebecca Bowens child of Patsey Bowens a child of colour aged about five years" under the tutelage of James Powell in order to learn "Farming." If the court failed to apprentice

---

[69] 1850 U. S. Federal Census, Hertford County, North Carolina.
[70] Hertford County Guardian Accounts, Volume 1, 109, 111-113, SANC.

girls to learn farm work, county officials usually assigned them to learn the work of a seamstress. Officials for the May 1832 court bound Liddy Bowser's daughter Mary to Miles H. Jernigan to learn this trade. Most girls like Mary Bowser could do little to improve their personal situation through such a common employment. On the other hand, boys who were not subjected to learn farming took on apprentice assignments that would allow them to practice a skilled trade. At the same session, the court bound "William Adkins child of Rachel Adkins 'a boy of colour'" to learn the more advanced art of "Boot & Shoemaking."[71]

White people in Hertford County not only valued free people of color for the work they performed but depended on them as an essential part of their business customer base. In a community in which so many people were enslaved and had limited access to money, free people of color were valuable customers for local white businessmen. White merchants such as Charles Vann profited through commerce with free people of color. Records show that Murphy Wyatt purchased tobacco, sugar, and coffee from Vann in 1842. During the same year, Hilary Nickens acquired buttons and thread at Vann's store. Thomas Weaver's 1843 account with Vann included orders for shoes, brandy, bacon, beef, a hat, blanket, and tobacco. On some occasions, free people of color failed to pay their credit account for the merchandise procured from Vann, and Vann took these debtors to court to seek redress. In 1843, Vann sued Paul and Sylvester Sears for a debt of $11.55. Later that year, Vann and his business partner G. W. Joyner took Edward Wiggins to court for $5.36 plus $3 damages; Hilary Nickens ended up in a similar position as the Searses and Wiggins. Unable to pay Vann in cash, Nickens surrender two barrels of corn, two tables, a bedstead, and a few other items in order to remunerate him.[72]

Similarly, white doctors such as Thomas O'Dwyer and John T. Lewter relied on business from free patients of color. In 1825, O'Dwyer

---

[71] Hertford County Court Minutes, Volume 2, 79, 98, SANC; Hertford County Court Minutes, Volume 1, February 1830, May 1830, February 1845, May 1832, SANC.
[72] Hilary Nickens Note May 2, 1842, Thomas Weaver Account 1843, *Vann v. Paul and Silvester Sears*, *Vann & Joyner v. Edward Wiggins*, Hilary Nickens Receipt, *Vann & Joyner v. Hillary Nickins*, Charles Vann Papers, Charles Vann Business Papers, Accounts, 1828-1867, ND, SANC.

traveled the county visiting patients and providing them with treatment. On several days in July of that year, he visited Jacob Boone, a free man of color who lay ill. The doctor kept close watch on his patient and supplied Boone with several prescriptions. During the same period, O'Dwyer also gave assistance to both Tryal Williamson and his wife, free people of color in need of medicine.[73] Additionally, Lewter cared for numerous free people of color around Murfreesboro. On several occasions, Lewter came to the aid of Benjamin and Mary Jones Reynolds's family. Several times in 1857, he supplied Mary and her daughter with medicines and ointments. The next year, Lewter performed surgery on Mary in order to remove a tumor from her breast. William C. Jones called on Lewter to set the broken forearm of his son Jimmy on June 10, 1859. During a January 14, 1860 visit to Andrew Reynolds's family, Lewter lanced an abscess on an infant. Several of the free families of color paid Lewter in cash for his services. Nevertheless, some could only reward him through barter. After visiting and providing medications for Preston, Uretta, and William Weaver, children of John and Sallie Keene Weaver, the family repaid Lewter by washing for him in 1859.[74]

Like other white businessmen, white lawyers developed commercial relationships with free people of color; they represented free people of color in court and assisted them with other legal matters. In the 1810s, Richard Nickens died leaving a wife and several adult children. The Nickens family depended on local attorney John Vann to administer Richard Nickens's significant estate which included both real and personal property. Vann took on the tedious task of tracking down and corresponding with Nickens's sons, who had left Hertford County for Tennessee, paying off Nickens's debts, and holding an estate sale.[75]

As members of the larger community in nineteenth-century Hertford County, free people of color were subjects of the county's court system. Free people of color came to the courthouse in Winton to conduct

---

[73] Thomas O'Dwyer Diary, July 6, 7, 8, 9, 11, 12, 13, 14, 15, 18, 20, 1825, SHC.
[74] John T. Lewter Ledger 1, 8, 40, 68, 136, J. T. Lewter Papers, Murfreesboro Historical Association Collection, East Carolina University Joyner Library.
[75] Richard Nickens Estate Papers, John Vann Papers, Estate Nickens, Richard 1815, SANC.

business. Those free people of color who bought or sold property registered their real estate transactions at the courthouse. After Margaret Hall transferred land to her son Andrew Hall, the Halls registered the deed with the court during May 1827. Furthermore, free people of color who administered estates had records related to the sales and distributions of those estates registered with the court. Serving as the administrator of Ezekiel Archer's estate, Simon Archer had the court clerk record the final settlement of the estate in May 1831. During August 1855, Jesse Keene recorded the sale of Tempy Nickens's estate with the court. Additionally, free people of color appeared in court to post bonds on behalf of friends and associates. Lawrence Weaver acted as a bondsman on behalf of his brother-in-law Allen Hall for a peace warrant. Moreover, widows came to court in order to petition for provisions from their husband's estates. During the February 1851 court session, Penny Bizzell Cotton requested provisions from the estate of her late husband Wiley Cotton. Free people of color also visited the court to request divisions of lands and estates. At the May 1858 session, Lawrence and Elihu Weaver petitioned the court for a land partition.[76]

In addition to handling business matters, Hertford County's free people of color commonly came to court to participate in litigation. They appeared as plaintiffs and defendants in civil trials in both upper and lower courts. In 1842, the county superior court heard the case of Henry Nickens, a free man of color, against William T. Bynum, a white man. At the conclusion of the trial, the court ruled in favor of Nickens and awarded him ten dollars damages. In 1849, Lemuel R. Jernigan, a white man, sued Jesse Reynolds, a free man of color, for "breach of contract." At the Spring 1850 term, the court found in favor of Reynolds and concluded that he "performed" the requirements of the contract. In Spring 1856, Nancy Hall Bailey, a free woman of color, sued her husband Alfred Bailey for divorce while Phillip Weaver, a free man of color, made the same filing

---

[76] Hertford County Record of Deeds, Volume L, 87-88, SANC; Hertford County Record of Estates, Volume 1, 129, SANC; Hertford County Record of Estates, Volume 3, 454, SANC; Hertford County Court Minutes, Volume 2, 434, SANC; Hertford County Court Minutes, Volume 4, 70, SANC.

Julia Bailey Jones was the only child of Alfred Bailey and Nancy Hall Bailey. In 1856, Julia's mother divorced her father. Later in her childhood, both of her parents remarried. Nancy Hall married Thomas Pierce, while Alfred Bailey had several other wives. As an adult, Julia married William W. Jones and had three sons: Willis E., Walter T., and John Pat. (Private Collection)

against his wife Lavinia. The next spring, jurors decided in favor of Nancy Hall Bailey and Phillip Weaver in their individual cases.[77]

Aside from civil cases, the local courts also took up cases against white defendants for committing crimes against free people of color. Unfortunately, most of the records describing the details of these cases have not survived. An account written by William D. Valentine in 1841, however, provides insight into one of these instances, a murder case prosecuted against an unnamed white man for the murder of "his wife who was a mulatto." Valentine explained, "Quite a strong circumstantial case was proved against him. But the witness on whose evidence the whole testimony depended, being an abandoned prostitute and common strumpet, the jury thought it not safe to hang a man on her evidence."[78]

Free persons of color regularly appeared in the courtroom as defendants in criminal cases. Although the minutes for the court that dealt with the most serious cases have failed to survive, other records clearly demonstrate that the court occasionally charged free people of color with the most serious crimes. In 1859, the court charged Henry Reynolds, a free

<hr>

[77] Hertford County Trial and Appearance Docket Superior Court, Volume 1, 66, 102, 105, 145, 153, SANC.
[78] William D. Valentine Diary, Volume 5, 45-46, SHC.

man of color, with the death of John Wiggins, another free person of color. An advertisement issued by the governor of North Carolina ordered that Reynolds, who was on the run, "be arrested and brought to trial." The governor's announcement described Reynolds as "about nineteen years of age, five feet two inches high, stands well on his feet and well formed, complexion a dingy mulatto, rather vicious countenance, and bears the marks upon his back of frequent whippings."[79]

The county's lower court, the Court of Pleas and Quarter Sessions, considered cases of less consequence than Henry Reynolds's situation. This court played a key role in the regulation of relationships between unmarried people. It heard several bastardy cases against free men of color accused of fathering children by unmarried women. On May 29, 1832, a jury concluded that Sylvester Sears, a free man of color, was the father of Eliza Lee's illegitimate child. The next year, the court required Harvey Hall, a free man of color, to pay child support to Sally Davis for a child she had delivered.[80] Cases concerning alleged inappropriate relationships between unmarried couples regularly appeared before the court. After hearing the case against them, jurors convicted William Futrell, a white man, and Frusa Reid, a free woman of color, of fornication and adultery on March 1, 1854.[81] The court also judged cases involving free people of color charged with minor violent crimes. During the November 1849 session, jurors listened to the case against Marina and David Melton, free persons of color, for an affray. After evaluating the evidence, the jury convicted David but absolved Marina. The court fined David one dollar and ordered him "to stand in the Pillory one hour." At the same court session, Rebecca Butler along with Martha and Lovey Melton all faced assault and battery charges. The jury in Butler's case convicted her, and the court levied a fine of five cents against her. Jurors in the Meltons' case, however, determined that Martha and Lovey were not guilty of assault and battery.[82] Small property criminal cases involving free people

[79] "$100 Reward," *Semi-Weekly Standard* (Raleigh), 12 March 1859.
[80] Hertford County Court Minutes, Volume 1, May 1832, May 1833, SANC.
[81] Hertford County Court Minutes, Volume 3, February 1854, SANC.
[82] Hertford County Court Minutes, Volume 2, 325-326, SANC.

of color also fell under the jurisdiction of the Court of Pleas and Quarter Sessions. On March 1, 1859, the court heard the case against Solomon Simmons, a free man of color, for petit larceny. At the conclusion of the case, the jury found Simmons guilty, and the court ordered that he "receive from the sheriff thirty lashes at the public whipping post" in addition to paying all court costs.[83]

Although the courts often worked in favor of free people of color, North Carolina law limited the legal rights of free people of color in certain situations and on rare, but noteworthy occasions, permitted the courts to punish convicted free people of color more harshly than white convicts. Since the 1750s, North Carolina prohibited free people of color from testifying against whites in court. The previously mentioned cases of Henry Nickens and Jesse Reynolds demonstrate that free people of color could win cases against their white neighbors without the privilege of testifying against them. The historical record, however, fails to speak to those cases in which the inability to testify may have challenged a free person of color's ability win or even wage a case.

During the nineteenth century, the state legislature passed a number of additional restrictions that applied to Hertford County's free people of color and others across the state. By the eve of the Civil War, state law prevented free people of color from retailing liquor, selling "goods, wares or commodities" outside of their home county, preaching, and carrying a gun or a series of other weapons without a license issued by their county court. The law also banned free persons of color from entering North Carolina if they were residents of another state or had left the state for a certain period of time. Legislators also approved a bill that allowed counties to hire out free people of color convicted of crimes and assess fines they could not pay. Of these discriminatory laws, the prohibition of testimony from free people of color against whites likely had the greatest impact. The act requiring a license to carry a gun also had widespread affects among free people of color as the Court of Pleas and Quarter Sessions heard many cases concerning free people of color allegedly carrying guns without licenses. At the May 1858 session, the jurors

---

[83] Hertford County Court Minutes, Volume 4, 119, SANC.

listened to the cases of John Hall, Mac Morris, Bolden Flood, John Carr, and Lewis Melton, all free men of color charged with carrying guns without licenses. A jury cleared John Hall of the charges while the court convicted the others and assessed fines against them. The same court also was in charge of issuing licenses to free people of color. The court granted weapons licenses good for up to a year. At the May 1859 session, the court granted permits to Smith Green, Wiley Garnes, Andrew Garnes, Preston Hall, Phillip Weaver, Josiah Flood, Meady Melton, and Stephen Archer. [84]

While managing a North Carolina county that bordered Virginia, Hertford County officials dealt with free people of color from Virginia illegally migrating into North Carolina. On some occasions, the county justices sought to prosecute these individuals for entering illegally. In his November 26, 1852 diary entry, William D. Valentine reported, "Many free negroes were indicted on presentment for emigrating [immigrating] into this state, into this county, Hertford from Virginia."[85] During the November 1857 session, the court charged John Hunt, a free man of color, with illegally coming into Hertford County. Hunt, however, failed to appear in court to face the charge.[86]

On rare occasions, convicted free people of color may have been subject to convict leasing. During the May 1833 session, a jury convicted Rachel Reynolds, a free woman of color, and two other women of an unspecified crime. The court fined one of the women "six pence," another "five dollars," and Reynolds "Twenty five dollars" and ordered that, "In the case Rachel Reynolds does not pay her fine & cost the Sheriff is directed to hire her out according to act of assembly."[87] The surviving record does not reveal whether Reynolds found a way to pay the fine or became a convict laborer. If she had connections to individuals who could loan her the money or if she had the money, Reynolds likely avoided hiring out. If Reynolds, however, was poor like the vast majority of free people of color, the sheriff likely hired her to one of her more affluent

---

[84] Hertford County Court Minutes, Volume 4, 66-67, 132, SANC.
[85] William D. Valentine Diary, Volume 12, 163, SHC.
[86] Hertford County Court Minutes, Volume 4, 20, SANC.
[87] Hertford County Court Minutes, Volume 1, May 1833, SANC.

neighbors. As a convict laborer, Reynolds would have worked under her master for up to five years.[88]

Well aware of the injustices in their state, Hertford County's free people of color took an active role in challenging attempts to curb their legal rights. After the North Carolina General Assembly passed an act in 1822 allowing slaves to testify against free people of color in criminal cases, fifty-two free men of color petitioned the legislature in protest of the new law. In their petition, these men highlighted that many of them had fought for American independence during the Revolution. They protested the idea of allowing enslaved people to testify against free people of color in court because of the power slave masters held over their bondspeople. These men asked the legislature "whether their situation even before the Revolution was not preferable to the one in which their dearest rights are held by so slight a tenure as the favour of slaves and the will & caprice of their vindictive masters for it cannot escape the notice of your Honorable Body that persons of this description are bound to a blind obedience, and know no Law, but the will of their masters."[89] The status of slaves in relation to their masters made their testimony against any free person a potential threat. By allowing slaves to testify against free people of color, the state legislature indirectly diminished the legal status of all free people of color and simultaneously affirmed the legal and political superiority of all whites regardless of their circumstances. The new law also increased the potential power and influence of the slaveholding class.

Living in a region with a slave-based economy, the petition's signers were well aware of the various extremes that could occur in relationships between bondspeople and masters. Many free people of color probably knew some enslaved individuals at a very personal level, and most knew their county's influential slaveholders. A few of Hertford County's free people of color actually owned slaves and understood slavery at its most

---

[88] *Acts Passed by the General Assembly of the State of North Carolina, at the Session of 1831-32* (Raleigh: Lawrence and Lemay, 1832), 12-13.
[89] The Petition of Sundry Persons of Colour of Hertford County Praying the Repeal of An Act of Last Session Declaring Slaves Competent Witnesses Against Free Persons of Colour, General Assembly Papers, Session Records, Miscellaneous Petitions, November-December 1822, Box 4, SANC.

fundamental level. Even if some of the signers maintained friendships with enslaved persons, they understood that those friendships were always maintained under the watchful eyes of slave masters and that those masters, armed with the chain and lash, had the ability to transform friends into enemies.

Hertford County's free men of color were not the only party to protest the legislature's attempt to compromise their legal status. Eighty-five white neighbors of the free men of color signed an adjoining petition supporting the protest of the free men of color. In their adjoining petition, the group of eighty-five contended that the new law "may in many cases be productive of the most serious mischief."[90] Many of the men who signed this petition were among the county's most influential and well-to-do slaveholders. Although, in theory, the law admitting slave testimony in cases against free people of color increased the influence of white men, these signers recognized that this new law was also a probable threat to the overall social order. The new law not only potentially increased the power of masters but also the power of slaves. This legislation created a fissure in the line between freedom and slavery by allowing slaves to participate in the courtroom as the co-equals of certain free persons and placed them on par with free citizens.

The signers of the adjoining petition also were likely concerned with the potential power this law gave to lower class whites; they understood that poor whites had the most to gain from the new law. When the signers claimed that "mischief" was a possible product of the new law, this is the class of people that most likely concerned them. Many of Hertford County's free people of color were more educated, more highly skilled, and had obtained more financial success than many of their white neighbors. The new law afforded poor whites a tool that gave them potential power over a group of people who in all measures except racial categorization were their social and economic betters. Poor whites could

---

[90] The Petition of Sundry Persons of Colour of Hertford County Praying the Repeal of An Act of Last Session Declaring Slaves Competent Witnesses Against Free Persons of Colour, General Assembly Papers, Session Records, Miscellaneous Petitions, November-December 1822, Box 4, SANC.

entice or force slaves to give false testimony against free persons of color without fear of adverse consequences; those slaves that could then testify against the most well-to-do free person of color could never give testimony against the poorest, most criminal white man or woman. Many wealthy whites in Hertford County depended upon tradesmen, farmers, and laborers, many of whom were free persons of color, for the goods and services that supported their businesses and plantations. They now had to tolerate the possibility that a poor white man or a slave now could fracture the economic system and destroy essential individuals within it.

With radical pro-slavery politicians seeking to limit their possibilities, the pre-Civil War nineteenth century was a period of both great successes and trying challenges for Hertford County's free people of color. In many ways, Hertford County residents incorporated free people of color into the larger community. Most of them lived in conditions much better than slaves and all had substantial legal rights. Free people of color often depended on one another during the most significant moments of their lives. Family and friends were at the core of their social lives. Although they lacked the privileges of wealthy white elites, free people of color were anything but slaves without masters. They operated with insight, intelligence, and skill, and even whites who sometimes scolded their presence had to admit their value to society.

# Chapter 3:
# The War of the Rebellion and Reconstruction

The outbreak of the Civil War, its conclusion, and the Reconstruction period that followed ushered in momentous changes for free people of color in Hertford County and across North Carolina. Although their legal status as free people would remain unchanged, the privileges available to them under their freedom fluctuated greatly throughout this time. During the Civil War, lawmakers and Confederate officials challenged the rights of free people of color to self-determination. They impressed them into their services and forced them to assist in their war to preserve slavery. Free people of color, however, fought back by running to the Union lines and finding protection under the federal forces. Many joined the U.S. army and helped put down the Confederate rebellion. After the war and the end of slavery, many of the individuals formerly categorized as "free people of color" used their education, wealth, and connections to help reinvent their society; these former free people of color participated in political, social, educational, and religious reforms. Although they were free before the war, they could do more with their liberty in the post-war society. Challenges from supporters of the old radical pro-slavery regime, however, limited their power. Public segregation between people of color and whites increased after the Civil War with the establishment of separate schools and the mass exodus of people of color from the white-dominated pre-Civil War era churches. Furthermore, some whites were willing to allow people of color to have some control over the affairs of people of color, but detested the idea that those same individuals of color would govern the lives of white people.

By 1860, the issue of slavery had fractured the nation politically, and pro-slavery forces in North Carolina's state legislature had enacted laws that whittled away many of the liberties of the free persons of color. These laws, however, generally failed to reshape fully the social position of free people of color in Hertford County, and many of the generations' old dependencies and relationships between free people of color and whites continued into the late antebellum era. The triumph of secessionist forces in the South during 1860 and 1861 brought the most significant alteration to these patterns. In 1861, the state legislature passed a law prohibiting free people of color from carrying fire arms. A few influential white people including Daniel Valentine, Lemuel R. Jernigan, Watson Lewis, and Miles Mitchell, all who maintained particularly close ties with free people of color, petitioned the assembly to rescind this law. The petition claimed that the law hampered local white jurists' ability to reward and maintain the support of free people of color, many who were likely more trustworthy than other whites in the county. In this case, the petitioners' efforts were unsuccessful.[91]

Legal injustices were followed by more brutish crimes as Confederate forces began to impress free people of color into the service of the secessionist regime. Eli Williamson, a sailor of color, served aboard the Curlew, a steamship that was converted into a Confederate war vessel, and was injured on that steamer during a battle.[92] The Confederates forced young men from their homes and required them to work on fortifications, drive wagons in supply trains, and complete other task related to their war effort. Wiley Reynolds remembered, "In 1861 or '62 I went to Roanoke Isl[an]d N.C., waited on Confederate officers."[93] Edwin Sears recalled that Confederate officials impressed him and other boys "to drive wagons from Winton to Boykins, Virginia." He also worked on the roads clearing ditches.[94] The Confederates took up James Turner and John Cumbo and

---

[91] Petition from Justices of the County Court of Hertford, General Assembly Session Records, August-September 1861, Box 4, Petitions (Aug.-Sept. 1861), SANC.

[92] Eli Williamson Soldier's Application for Pension, State Auditor Pension Office Confederate Pension Records/Applications for Pensions Act of 1901, Box 6.642, Williamson, Eli Hertford, SANC.

[93] William Weaver alias Wiley Reynolds Deposition October 31, 1902, William Weaver alias Wiley Reynolds Pension, Civil War Pensions, NARA.

[94] "Interview with Edwin Sears," E. Franklin Frazier Papers Box 131–92, Folder 7; Manuscript Division, Moorland-Spingarn Research Center, Howard University.

During the Civil War, John B. Collins, son of William Collins and Jane Bizzell Collins, escaped to the Union lines and joined the 14th U.S. Colored Heavy Artillery. After the war, he became active in the Republican Party and campaigned on behalf of President Ulysses Grant. (Private Collection)

forced them to work in the part of Hertford County known as "Pitch Landing" packing pork and beef for the Confederate army.[95]

Many young free men of color resisted the Confederate demands and absconded from their imposed duties. After returning home for a Christmas break, Edwin Sears decided not to continue with the Confederates; he left his mother's house and hid out in the woods at the home of his sister. The Confederates tried to retrieve Sears, but they could not find him. Edwin eventually met up with his cousins John B. Collins, Simon P. Collins, and John Smith and escaped to the Union lines.[96] While working at Pitch Landing, John Cumbo and James Turner also found the opportunity to run to the Union forces. James Turner recalled, "a Federal Captain and his soldiers took them to Roanoke Island." They eventually landed in Union-controlled New Bern.[97] Matthew Walden, Thomas Reynolds, and several others made a similar escape. Walden stated, "29 of us ran away from Hertford Co NC to get to the Union lines. It was in Feb[ruar]y 1864 and we were about 3 weeks getting to Plymouth NC about 60 miles from Hertford Co NC. I remember we came on a boat called the 'Bombshell' from Catherine Creek on the Chowan River to Plymouth NC and we went to Newbern NC by boat."[98]

After Abraham Lincoln's decision to raise colored regiments, Hertford County's free men of color received the opportunity to support the effort against the rebellion by joining the Union Army. Most of Hertford County's free men of color who enlisted in the federal forces served with the 35th, 36th, or 37th U.S. Colored Infantries, 14th U.S. Colored Heavy Artillery, or the 2nd U.S. Colored Calvary. A few enlisted with other army outfits or joined the navy. Many families committed several sons to the Union war effort. William T., Elvey D. James A., and

---

[95] James J. Baker Deposition October 21, 1872, James Turner Deposition November 13, 1873, John Cumbo Pension, Civil War Pensions, NARA.

[96] "Interview with Edwin Sears," E. Franklin Frazier Papers Box 131–92, Folder 7; Manuscript Division, Moorland-Spingarn Research Center, Howard University.

[97] James Turner Deposition November 13, 1873, John Cumbo Pension, Civil War Pensions, NARA.

[98] Mathew Walden Deposition September 26, 1892, Thomas Reynolds Pension, Civil War Pensions, NARA.

Joshua Nickens (standing on the right) served in the U.S. Navy during the Civil War. After the war, Nickens left Hertford County and lived as a white man in New York. He is pictured with his wife Bessie Gilligan Nickens (seated to the right) and friends Patrick Layden (standing on the left) and Catherine Smith (seated on the left). (National Archives and Records Administration)

Giles A. Lewis, sons of Elvey and Frances Manley Lewis, all enlisted in the Union Army. Benjamin and Amelia Hall Weaver's children Edward, William A., and John Thomas Weaver left home to help put down the rebellion. Cousins Joshua Nickens, Thomas Weaver, and Lawrence E. Weaver departed Hertford County and joined the Union Navy.[99]

Upon their enlistments, free men of color underwent close examinations by military doctors. On arrival in New Bern, Alfred Bailey recalled, "I was stripped and physically examined by two doctors and sworn in."[100] Bryant Manley described that he "was stripped and examined when he entered the service and pronounced sound by the surgeon."[101] John Thomas Weaver provided a more detailed account of his physical: "I was stript [stripped] naked and examined at my enlistment— the doctor seemed to examine me at every part…He thumped me in [the] breast, side and back…He measured me for my height."[102]

Free men of color took on a variety of tasks while in the service of the United States. Wiley Reynolds recalled that upon his enlistment, "they put a rifle in my hand and drilled me."[103] The army set many free men of color to manual labor. Hampton Reynolds explained, "I was in camp at Atlantic City near Fort Macon N.C. in 1864 we built barracks & houses & had to carry pine poles on our shoulders for ¼ & more miles."[104] Lawrence E. Weaver remembered, "I enlisted at Plymouth, N.C. Jan 19th 1864 as [a] 1st class boy. I went out and staid [stayed] a couple of days on the receiving

---

[99] Sally J. Lewis Deposition November 10, 1902, William T. Lewis Pension, Civil War Pensions, NARA; Elvey Lewis Deposition September 10, 1902, Elvey Lewis Pension, Civil War Pensions, NARA; John T. Weaver Deposition February 3, 1897, James A. Lewis Deposition February 3, 1897, William A. Weaver Deposition June 1, 1897, John T. Weaver Pension, Civil War Pensions, NARA; Lawrence E. Weaver Deposition January 9, 1893, Lawrence E. Weaver Pension, Civil War Pensions, NARA.
[100] Alfred Bailey Deposition October 16, 1900, Alfred Bailey Pension, Civil War Pensions, NARA.
[101] Bryant Manley Affidavit December 9, 1889, Bryant Manley Pension, Civil War Pensions, NARA.
[102] John T. Weaver Deposition February 3, 1897, John T. Weaver Pension, Civil War Pensions, NARA.
[103] William Weaver alias Wiley Reynolds Deposition October 31, 1902, William Weaver alias Wiley Reynolds Pension, Civil War Pensions, NARA.
[104] Hampton Reynolds Affidavit May 11, 1896, Hampton Reynolds Pension, Civil War Pensions, NARA.

ship 'Southfield' and about the 21$^{st}$ Jan 1864 I went aboard the USS 'Miami' and staid [stayed] on her until I was transferred on board the USS 'Constellation' sometime in May 1865 & staid [stayed] on her until I was discharged at Norfolk Navy Yard."[105] James Reid recalled, "I knew the soldier John Weaver before the war. I went to the Yankee army with him and we came back together. I waited on Capt. Tom Maher Co. B 14 U.S.C.H. Art., and John Weaver was a soldier."[106]

In the process of working to break the Confederacy, a few young men lost their lives, most of these few dying of disease, while several became sick or were injured in combat. John C. Reynolds came down with consumption and died in New Bern on July 29, 1864.[107] While serving with the 35$^{th}$ U.S. Colored Infantry, George Archer caught an unknown disease and died of diarrhea on August 18, 1864 in Jacksonville, Florida. On August 15, 1865, Enoch Luton, a free man of color from Hertford County, wrote to Nancy Ann Weaver Walden informing her of her husband's death. Writing from Fort Macon, North Carolina, he explained, "I now seat myself as to let you know that I am in common health and all of the Boys that are living. Richard R. Weaver are dead and your Husband Samuel Walden also. He lived about a month after he got to the regiment. He died with the tiford disentary [typhoid dysentery]. He requested that I should write to you."[108] Lemuel Reynolds survived the war but injured himself while on fatigue duty. He recalled, "I received a severe hurt which caused the rupture. I was sent to [the] hospital (regimental) & remain there about one week. So many folks were dying in there I left there & went back to my company—would rather suffer there than to be in [the] hospital."[109] Bryant Manley became ill while in the service. Speaking of

---

[105] Lawrence E. Weaver Deposition January 9, 1893, Lawrence E. Weaver Pension, Civil War Pensions, NARA.
[106] James Reid Deposition October 13, 1903, John Weaver Pension, Civil War Pensions, NARA.
[107] Adjutant General's Office Report September 19, 1871, John C. Reynolds Pension, Civil War Pensions, NARA.
[108] Enoch Luton to Nancy Walden August 15, 1865, Samuel Walden Pension, Civil War Pensions, NARA.
[109] Lemuel Reynolds Affidavit August 24, 1892, Lemuel Reynolds Pension, Civil War Pensions, NARA.

During the Civil War, Nancy Ann Weaver Walden lost her husband Samuel Walden, a Union soldier, to disease. She later married Peter Hunter of Nansemond County, Virginia. (Private Collection)

his brother Bryant's condition, Wilson Manley indicated, "The first I knew there was anything the matter with him was in Dec 1864 at Carolina City N.C. he was then down with the neuralgia in [the] head & rheumatism in [the shoulders]. The surgeon pulled some of his teeth to relieve this neuralgia in his face, as his face was very much swollen."[110] Thomas M. Collins was one of the few free people of color to become wounded in battle. One of his comrades indicated that Collins "got wounded by a ball striking him in the right foot" near Cold Harbor, Virginia.[111]

Despite the pressure of war, many of Hertford County's free men of color who enlisted sought to make their situations as normal as possible by focusing on family life and socialization. Dempsey Newsome who was based in New Bern had his family join him there. His daughter Martha recalled, "During the war I went to Newberne N.C. where my father was in the 14th U.S.C.H.A. Co C."[112] While stationed with the army, James Smith, who was enlisted with the 14th U.S. Colored Heavy Artillery, married Mary Eliza Carey, a Hertford County native, at New Bern. Mary recollected, "We lived together as man and wife all the rest of the time the regiment was at Newberne. Just at discharge, maybe a month before, I came back home in a family way."[113] Playing sports was a common way to socialize and exercise during breaks from duty. Richard H. Weaver recalled that he and his comrades at Fort Macon played a game called "base." He explained that during a game of base, "we would have a base and one soldier would lead off from his base and another from [the] opposite base would run after to catch him."[114]

Those free people of color who remained on the home front attempted to keep their lives as normal as possible with differing degrees of success.

---

[110] Wilson Manley Deposition July 1, 1890, Bryant Manley Pension, Civil War Pensions, NARA.

[111] Justin C. Belknap Affidavit February 21, 1893, Thomas M. Collins Pension, Civil War Pensions, NARA.

[112] Mary Cumbo (Martha Cumbo) Deposition July 19, 1894, James Smith Pension, Civil War Pensions, NARA.

[113] Mary Eliza Lewis Deposition July 18, 1894, James Smith Pension, Civil War Pensions, NARA.

[114] Richard Weaver to Commissioner of Pensions July 13, 1885, Elvey Lewis Pension, Civil War Pensions, NARA.

Martha Newsome was the daughter of Dempsey Newsome and Elizabeth Manley Newsome. During the Civil War, she traveled with her family to New Bern while her father was stationed there with the 14th U.S. Colored Heavy Artillery. After the war, Martha returned to Hertford County, married William Cumbo, and raised a large family. (Private Collection)

During the war, those free people of color excluded from Confederate impressment or living beyond the Union camps continued with their regular activities. Farmers and laborers remained in the fields planting and plowing. Men, women, and children maintained their attendance at churches and schools. Young couples courted and married. The poor, elderly, and crippled all continued to struggle to make ends meet.

Union movements through Hertford County, however, sometimes disrupted the normal patterns of life for free people of color. John Reid decided to join a group of Union troops as they moved through his community. He recalled, "In April 1865, a large body of United States soldiers came along going towards Jackson N.C. & when they passed my house, they compel[l]ed me to go with them to Jackson."[115] Eli Williamson, who returned home after receiving an injury in battle, described an encounter with Union troops passing through his neighborhood: "Sometime in July 1863, Gen[era]ls Hackman & Potter landed a large force of soldiers both cavalry & artillery at Winton N.C. & remained about 5 days. They went through the county on a raid. I lived about 5 ½ miles from Winton, & some of the soldiers went to my house, & told my wife that they wanted my horse…She told them that I did not have but one, & beg[g]ed them not to take him." Nevertheless, the soldier seized the horse but promised to return him. They, however, failed to fulfill that promise.[116]

The efforts of many of Hertford County's free people of color along with thousands of other Americans eventually led to the fall of the Confederate regime in 1865. Swift actions by the Republican-led Congress temporarily diminished the power and control of the surviving conservative elite. After the Civil War, free people of color in Hertford County and around the state could once again partake in the electoral franchise. They participated in political organizing in Hertford County and across the state while several also ran for and secured political office.

---

[115] John Reid Deposition, William B. Howard Claim, Southern Claims Commission Records, NARA.

[116] Ely Williamston Deposition, Ely Williamson Claim, Southern Claims Commission Records, NARA.

Simon P. Collins, son of William Collins and Jane Bizzell Collins, served with the 14th U.S. Colored Heavy Artillery during the Civil War. Following the Confederate surrender, he became active in Republican Party politics. (Private Collection)

Experience with and likely some understanding of electoral politics gained during the pre-war days seemingly provided them with a step up in Hertford County politics.

Former free people of color bolstered Republican politics in Hertford County during the post-Civil War nineteenth century. William David Newsome, Lemuel Washington Boone, John T. Reynolds, Andrew Reynolds, Joseph P. Weaver, David D. Weaver, William C. Jones, Osborn A. Giles, Simon P. Collins, John B. Collins, John "Jack" Bizzell, Jr., Joseph B. Catus, and Phillip Weaver participated in coordinating for the Republican Party. Soon after the end of the Civil War, these men and others began to organize people in support of the Republicans.

By 1867, former free men of color were active in political organizing at the local level. In that year, the Republican Party's State Executive Committee appointed Osborn A. Giles, John Bizzell, Jr., Phillip Weaver, and William Reid, all former free persons of color, to serve as the County Executive Committee for Hertford County. These men were in charge of supervising Republican affairs in the county, appointing precinct committees within the county, and calling county-level party conventions. On August 1, 1867, Republican organizers brought together between 2,500 and 3,000 people in Murfreesboro to celebrate the anniversary of emancipation in the West Indies. At the event, William Reid served as chairman and president while the secretary, John T. Reynolds, helped call the crowd to order. Andrew Reynolds led the crowd in prayer during the event.[117]

Former free people of color also participated in Republican Party events of statewide and national significance. Before the 1868 election, several of these men led a Grant and Colfax Meeting in Winton in support of Ulysses Grant for president of the United States and Schuyler Colfax for vice president. At the meeting, W. D. Newsome served as chairman with John T. Reynolds as secretary. Lemuel Washington Boone and John B. Collins spoke along with C. L. Cobb of Elizabeth City, who was the

---

[117] "Republican Platform," *The Daily Standard* (Raleigh), 14 May 1868; "Republican Celebration of the First of August in Murfreesborough," *The Weekly Standard* (Raleigh), 14 August 1867.

William Reid was a political and religious leader in post-Civil War Hertford County. He was a minister and served as a county commissioner, magistrate, Republican Party organizer, and trustee of Waters Normal Institute. (Private Collection)

keynote speaker. The meeting's attendees passed several resolutions including an endorsement of Grant and Colfax for president and vice president, a pledge of continued support for the Republican Party, and a denunciation of the Democratic Party, whom they predicted "would inaugurate their course by using whatever means within their power to snatch from the newly enfranchised race of the South the ballot."[118] The 1868 election was a success for the Grant and Colfax ticket along with several of its supporters in Hertford County. W. D. Newsome and William Reid both secured spots on the county board of commissioners. During the same election, John T. Reynolds won a contest to represent neighboring Northampton. In the following election, Newsome would move up to the state house of representatives.[119]

Nevertheless, by the mid-1870s, conservative Democrats wrestled away influence from the Republicans in North Carolina and eventually would do exactly what the attendees of the Hertford County Grant and Colfax meeting foresaw. The Democrats, however, would not dominate state and local politics until the turn of the century, and Republicans of color and their allies continued to operate in Hertford County with some level of success during the period before the Democratic Party ascendancy. In 1874, W. D. Newsome chaired a Republican Convention for the county at the courthouse in Winton. David D. Weaver acted as the convention secretary, and Lemuel Washington Boone participated as the main speaker at the event. The convention nominated Newsome as its candidate for the state house of representatives. Members of the convention appointed William C. Jones of Murfreesboro District and John "Jack" Bizzell, Jr. of Saint John's District among others as delegates for the convention's nominating committee. William Reid, whom the delegates chose to run for the county commission, was the only former free person of color nominated by the committee.[120]

---

[118] "Grant and Colfax Meeting in Hertford," *The Weekly Standard* (Raleigh), 19 August 1868.
[119] "Official," *The Daily Standard* (Raleigh), 21 May 1868.
[120] "Republican Convention in Hertford County," *The Weekly Era* (Raleigh), 23 July 1874.

Lemuel Washington Boone risked his life to fight for and provide people of color in eastern North Carolina with political rights, education, and religious autonomy. Boone founded churches and assisted in the establishment of several organizations. He was also active in Republican politics and ran for public office. Several of his descendants followed his example by becoming noteworthy figures in religion, education, and civic leadership. (Private Collection)

On the eve of Democratic domination of North Carolina politics during the latter part of the century and early part of the 1900s, a few former free people of color continued to hold political positions. Through the 1890s, several of them held appointments as judges of elections including Arthur Reynolds, Andrew Jackson Archer, Joseph H. Archer, Eff Richard Jones, John W. Weaver, and William C. Jones. In 1889, George W. Reynolds accepted an appointment as postmaster for Murfreesboro. Samuel Weaver was the constable in Winton during the late 1890s. In 1895, the state legislature appointed William Reid as a magistrate for Murfreesboro and Isaiah Boone as a magistrate for Winton. Joseph B. Catus, who served as a justice of the peace and postmaster of Winton until his death in 1913, was one of the last people of color in North Carolina to hold public office before the exclusion of people of color from public office during the Jim Crow period. He also represented Hertford County at multiple Republican conventions including those held in 1888 and 1900.[121]

---

[121] "Commissioners Court," *Murfreesboro Index*, 10 October 1890; "Commissioners Court," *Murfreesboro Index*, 7 October 1892; "Judges of Election," *Murfreesboro Index*,

The former free persons of color who participated in political activities operated within an environment in which they experienced many successes; yet their enemies always sought to keep them at bay. From the conclusion of the Civil War, conservatives sought to use terror and violence to dissuade and punish free people of color who challenged white supremacy. Returning home from military duty, free people of color faced attacks from supporters of the old order. In 1866, John "Jack" Bizzell, Jr., Andrew J. Reynolds, James Manley, Bryant Manley, Richard H. Weaver, and Miles Weaver reported harassment from local whites on their return home after completing their service with the U.S. military to the Freedmen's Bureau. They explained that a militia forced them to surrender their guns upon their arrival in the county. Bizzell also stated that several men under the command of Jesse Sewell entered his house and plundered it during the night.[122] Likewise, extremists targeted Lemuel Washington Boone and attempted to assault him in 1868. John T. Reynolds informed Freedmen's Bureau officials that William Lawrence led an attack in which the assailants pulled "knives and pistols" on Boone.[123] Ten years later, an unidentified party burned down a building owned by W. D. Newsome. A local newspaper recounted that the store building had "been used since the 1st of June every Saturday night for the meeting of a colored debating society…this debating society has finally developed a political League, and a meeting of this nature had just terminated when the fire was discovered."[124] Former free people of color and their allies risked their lives in order to have a political voice in Hertford County.

---

28 October 1896; "Locals," *Murfreesboro Index*, 8 November 1889; "County Commissioners," *Murfreesboro Index*, 11 December 1896; "New Magistrates," *Murfreesboro Index*, 22 March 1895; "Republican Congressional Convention," *The North Carolinian* (Elizabeth City), 29 August 1888; "Proceeding of the Republican Congressional Convention—Second Meeting," *The North Carolinian* (Elizabeth City), 21 June 1900.

[122] Letter from John Bizzell and others, Records of the Field Offices for the State of North Carolina, Bureau of Refugees, Freedmen, and Abandoned Lands, 1865-1872, M1909, Roll 35, NARA.

[123] Register of Letters Received, Volume 3, March-December 1868, Records of the Assistant Commissioner for the State of North Carolina, Bureau of Refugees, Freedmen, and Abandon Lands, 1862-1870, M843, Roll 6, NARA.

[124] "Store House Burned," *The Albemarle Enquirer* (Murfreesboro), 14 November 1878.

Brothers Preston D. Manley (left) and George D. Manley (right) worked as loggers through the early twentieth century. Preston D. Manley is pictured with his wife, Armittie Simmons Manley, and child. (Private Collections)

The former free people of color played a critical role in Hertford County's everyday workings beyond formal politics. Through the last decades of the nineteenth century, they continued to be influential in the local economy and helped fulfill the needs of their neighbors. Farming remained a key occupation during this period while many former free people of color worked in the fishing industry. During the 1870s, Wiley Jones, James Manley, John Reynolds, John Manley, George Keene, Simon Bizzell, James Henry Nickens, Nathaniel "Nat" Turner, Joseph Reynolds, James Starkey Pugh, and William Weaver were among the many individuals employed at the local fisheries. They rigged nets in preparation for making large catches and fished the waters. Some fishermen traveled significant distances to find their catches. A few years after the Civil War, John Thomas Weaver and Wilson Chavis worked together as fishermen on Albemarle Sound. Former free people of color performed many other types of work beyond fishing and farming. William Overton and Elvey D. Lewis labored as ditch diggers. William Trotman Weaver was a sailor. Additionally, former free people of color played a key role in the logging industry in Hertford County. Brothers Preston D. and George D. Manley cut timber through the early twentieth century.[125]

Some of the work performed by former free people of color was not as physically intensive as farm work and other forms of heavy labor. The development of schools for people of color during Reconstruction created an increased demand for teachers in the county. Former free people of color like Emanuel Reynolds attended to the religious and ceremonial needs of the community. Through the latter part of the century, Reynolds performed weddings and preached at funerals. In addition to educators and clergy, a few former free people of color owned businesses. Richard Wiggins, Arrajah Smith, and Eff Richard Jones managed general stores in Cofield and Winton. Nancy Jones Turner was the proprietor of a restaurant in Winton. Eli Williamson operated a distillery. Several jobs that supported the Hertford County community were performed primarily by women. Women such as Jane Bizzell Collins administered home remedies to the sickly. Many women aided their sisters, daughters, neighbors, and friends with the deliveries of their children. Some women worked in less-respected occupations. In 1870, the census taker listed Kittie Flood as a "prostitute."[126]

Following the Civil War, former free people of color and whites maintained the old business and social patterns of the past. They continued to live interdependent lives in which former free people of color and whites lived as neighbors, conducted business with one another, and supported one another in times of need. Samuel Jordan Wheeler, a local white planter and doctor, interacted regularly with former free people of

---

[125] Petty Shore Fishery Ledger, Wynn Family Papers, SANC; William Overton Affidavit, Elvey Lewis Pension, Civil War Pensions, NARA; John W. Weaver Deposition December 12, 1917, James Walden Pension, Civil War Pensions, NARA; Wilson Chavers Deposition February 3, 1897, John Thomas Weaver Deposition February 3, 1897, John T. Weaver Pension, Civil War Pensions, NARA; 1900 U.S. Federal Census, First Division Winton Township, Hertford County, North Carolina.
[126] Pennie A. Holleman Deposition April 23, 1902, Richard Wiggins Deposition April 24, 1902, Lemuel W. Weaver Pension, Civil War Pensions, NARA; Lawrence E. Weaver Deposition January 9, 1893, Lawrence E. Weaver Pension, Civil War Pensions, NARA; Levi Branson and Myrtle C. Branson, ed., *Branson's North Carolina Business Directory 1890* (Raleigh: Levi Branson, 1889), 366-368.

The Floods and the Meltons were two of the many farming families in late nineteenth-century Hertford County. During the period, agriculture was the primary way families survived and made a living. They grew produce to feed themselves and cash crops for the market. Benjamin Flood, son of Josiah Flood and Abscilla Archer Flood, and Mary Eliza Reid Flood, daughter of John Reid and Francis Wiggins Reid, are pictured at the top. Richard P. Melton and Calcey D. Melton, children of Wiley Melton and Rebecca Melton, appear at the bottom. (Private Collection)

color as his business dealings often included them. On numerous occasions in the first couple of years after the war, Wheeler sent shoes and boots to the shoemaker Calvin Weaver for repairs while Charles Simmons cut wood for him. In late August 1865, Andrew Reynolds sent his daughter to deliver peaches and eggs to Wheeler. During a visit to Winton in 1866, Wheeler procured apples from Wiley Jones. He also provided his neighbors of color with services. In December 1865, he assisted Cordelia Weaver with her dental issues by pulling one of her teeth. Although business interactions were an important facet of Wheeler's relationships with former free people of color, he also socialized with them. Former free people of color such as William C. Jones, John T. Reynolds, and Andrew Reynolds visited the Wheeler home to sing with his family. Former free persons of color frequently sought advice or assistance from Wheeler. After the arrest of Ann Weaver for allegedly stealing cabbages, her sister Frances approached Wheeler about helping to get Ann out of the situation. After Sunday dinner on March 28, 1866, Wheeler discussed the operations of the Sunday school for people of color with George Worrell and former free men of color William C. Jones and Andrew Reynolds. Later that year, Andrew Reynolds returned to him to chat about "church difficulties."[127]

During the Reconstruction period, many former free people of color assisted with Hertford County's system of law and order. By 1868, they started to serve as jurors during trials. That year, two of them, Preston Reynolds and Jack Butler, helped decide a suit that Meady Melton, a former free person of color, waged against Horatio Hays, a white man. These men along with their fellow jurors decided in favor of Melton.[128] Former free persons of color also participated in juries for coroner's inquests. In 1867, Lawrence Weaver, William T. Lewis, Smith Green, William H. Hall, John Reynolds, Theophilus Jordan, Ashley Melton, Thomas Boone, Mills Melton, Theophilus Trummell, Lewis Boone, and Giles A. Lewis joined the county coroner George W. Wynns in an attempt to determine Peggy Anderson's cause of death. They concluded that

[127] Samuel Jordan Wheeler Diary, Volume 2, 85, 87-88, 115, 120, SHC; Samuel Jordan Wheeler Diary, Volume 3, 55-56, 62, 69, 106, SHC.
[128] Hertford County Superior Court Minute Docket, Volume 1, 5, SANC.

John T. Reynolds was a leader in politics, religion, and education during the second half of the nineteenth century. Reynolds was a member of the North Carolina General Assembly, served as a trustee for Shaw University, and held leadership roles in several other organizations. (State Archives of North Carolina)

Anderson came to her end by "falling into the fire."[129] In an 1880 case, Benjamin Weaver, Charles Weaver, Preston Reynolds, Willis Weaver, James Butler, John P. Butler, James Chavis, William Trotman Weaver, and Thomas Weaver along with other neighbors examined the body of Andrew Lang. After inspecting the scene of the death and speaking with Lang's wife Rotha, the jurors and coroner agreed that "Andrew Lang came to his death by his own hands and with his own razor."[130] On the rare occasions in which they occurred, former free people of color helped evaluate cases involving alleged insane persons. During 1894, the county charged W. D. Newsome and Joseph P. Weaver along with a white local doctor, S. S. Daniel, to determine the fitness of Rosa Jones Pierce. Following their examination of Pierce, the men decided she was "insane" and recommended her removal to the insane asylum, "The Eastern Hospital," in Goldsboro, North Carolina.[131]

During Reconstruction, former free persons of color appeared in the local courts as plaintiffs and defendants in numerous cases. Unlike in the first part of the nineteenth-century, however, they had increased legal protections in those cases. Other people of color could now serve in the juries who heard their cases. The state had abolished the laws prohibiting their testimony against whites.

Former free people of color were involved in a variety of common civil disputes such as divorce throughout the period. In 1873, Sarah Pugh Simmons filed for divorce from her husband of less than five years Samuel Simmons. In her statement against Samuel, Sarah claimed that her husband had inflicted "repeated whippings" and "cruel treatment generally" upon her. Furthermore, she declared that Samuel hated her "as bad as a rattle snake, and that she might as well go to, or be in hell, as to

---

[129] Peggy Anderson Inquest, Hertford County Miscellaneous Records, Box 1, Coroners' Inquests, 1866-1908, SANC.
[130] Inquest over Andrew Lang, Hertford County Miscellaneous Records, Box 1, Coroners' Inquests, 1866-1908, SANC.
[131] Rosa Jones Lunacy Inquisition, Hertford County Miscellaneous Records, Box 2, Lunacy Inquests, 1865-1898, SANC.

live with him."[132] Ultimately a jury denied Sarah's petition and ruled in favor of her husband.[133] James H. Lee made his 1883 divorce case against his wife Amanda Luton Lee on different grounds and found a different result in the court. He complained Amanda had committed adultery with various men including Solomon Keene and George W. Collins. In addition, James explained that only a little more than a year after their marriage Amanda gave "birth to a bastard child." He knew the child did not belong to him because Amanda had "abandoned" him "about eleven and one half months" before the child's birth. In this case, the jury sided with the plaintiff and granted the divorce petition.[134]

Bastardy cases were another type of case former free persons of color commonly found themselves involved in. Women pursued these cases against men they alleged fathered their children outside of wedlock. On September 28, 1878, Margaret Brown came to court and confessed that Horatio Mitchell was the father of her eight-month-old son. Upon his appearance in court, Mitchell admitted to fathering Margaret Brown's son. The court awarded Brown $12 and required Mitchell to provide her with $10 per year child support for six years. In a similar case, a pregnant Ella B. Manley pointed to Delno Hall when court officials requested her to provide the name of the man who impregnated her. On September 9, 1893, after hearing the case, the court ordered the teenage Delno Hall to pay a fine of $10 and all court costs. Delno was also responsible for paying Manley $50 in installments and posting $200 for the maintenance of the child. His brother Albert Valentine Hall and brother-in-law William Beverly Weaver assisted him in producing the bond money.[135]

---

[132] *Sarah Simmons v. Samuel Simmons*, Hertford County Divorces, Box 2, Sarah Simmons v Samuel Simmons, 1873, SANC.

[133] Hertford County Superior Court Minute Docket, Volume 1, 68, SANC.

[134] *James H. Lee v. Amanda Luton*, Hertford County Divorces, Box 1, James H. Lee vs. Amanda Lee, 1883, SANC.

[135] *State and Margaret Brown v. Horatio Mitchell*, Hertford County Bastardy Bonds and Records, Box 1, Bastardy Bonds and Records, 1877-1878, SANC; Hertford County Superior Court Minute Docket, Volume 1, 227, SANC; *State and Ella B. Mandly v. Delno Hall*, Hertford County Bastardy Bonds and Records, Box 1, Bastardy Bonds and Records, 1887-1898, SANC.

The courts were regularly involved in land divisions and disputes among former free persons of color. The case concerning the division of Andrew Hall's land is one notable case. In 1884, siblings Preston Hall and Ophelia Hall Reynolds along with Ophelia's husband Alfred sued their aunt Amelia Hall Weaver's children, William, Martha, and John Thomas, their uncles Allen and Harvey Hall, their brother-in-law Joseph Chavis, and A. C. Vann, who purchased part of Allen Hall's interest, for the sale of the 100 acres once owned by Andrew Hall, the brother of their mother Penny Hall. Preston, Ophelia, and Alfred contended that the land could not be divided "without great damage to and materially affecting the interests of the owners of the shares" and requested the sale on those grounds.[136]

The local courts heard the cases of numerous former free people of color charged with an assortment of minor crimes during the Reconstruction period. During the Fall 1868 term of Superior Court, a grand jury presented Ann Weaver "for stealing Berry Vaughan's potatoes."[137] In Weaver's case, the court found the defendant guilty.[138] During Fall 1887 court, grand jurors charged Martha Keene with keeping "a disorderly and ill-governed house." At this location, she allegedly "then and there unlawfully cause and procure for her own lucre and gain, certain persons as well men as women, of evil name and fame, and of dishonest conversation to frequent and come together in said house, at unlawful times as well in the night as in the day, and did permit them then and there to be and remain drinking and tippling, whoring and misbehaving themselves, to the great damage of the public peace and good order."[139] In 1896, a grand jury indicted Mollie Garnes for a breach of contract after receiving a complaint from William A. Chavis. Chavis contended that Garnes "unlawfully and with intent to cheat and defraud" him "did obtain from him…one dollar in money, two pair of shoes, day goods and other thing to the amount of twenty five dollars" under a promise that she

---

[136] *Hall et als v. Vann et als*, Hertford County Civil and Criminal Action Papers, Box 6, Preston Hall et als vs. William Weaver et als, 1884, SANC.
[137] *Stave v. Ann Weaver*, Hertford County Civil and Criminal Action Papers, Box 3, Civil and Criminal Cases, 1868 (4), SANC.
[138] Hertford County Superior Court Minute Docket, Volume 1, 9, SANC.
[139] *State v. Martha Keen*, Hertford County Miscellaneous Records, SANC.

"would commence or begin to labor on his farm during the year 1896."
Yet, according to Chavis, Garnes failed "to begin and complete" the work
"without a lawful excuse." At trial, the jury sided with Garnes. Chavis
appealed to the higher court.[140]

On rare occasions, former free persons of color appeared in court
charged with murder. Rocius Trummell and William Crockett Reynolds
both found themselves in this position during the late-nineteenth century.
During the Fall 1881 session of Superior Court, a grand jury charged
Rocius Trummell with the murder of Peter Taylor, a man of color. The
indictment against Trummell alleged that he "did strike & beat" Taylor
with a plank, which produced a "mortal wound" to his head.[141] Trummell,
however, avoided justice. After the murder took place, the sheriff failed to
locate Trummell, and the prosecutor ultimately dropped the case.[142] In the
1893 indictment of William Crockett Reynolds, grand jurors claimed
Reynolds viciously killed his stepfather Henry Harrison. After hearing
testimony from several individuals, a jury exonerated Reynolds of the
murder.[143]

After the Civil War, former free people of color played an imperative
role in the formation and operations of new religious institutions. They
helped establish several new congregations including Philippi Baptist
Church, Newsome Grove Baptist Church, and First Baptist Church of
Murfreesboro. Religious leaders Lemuel Washington Boone, Emanuel
Reynolds, and William Reid organized churches, ministered to
congregations, participated in religious organizations, and wed couples
around the region. Immediately following the war, Boone led an exodus of
parishioners of color from the Meherrin Baptist Church to the newly
formed First Colored Baptist Church in Murfreesboro (First Baptist
Church of Murfreesboro). Reid followed Boone as pastor at First Baptist

---

[140] *State and William A. Chavis v. Molly Garnes*, Hertford County Miscellaneous
Records, SANC.
[141] *State v. Rocius Trummell*, Hertford County Civil and Criminal Action Papers, Box 5,
State vs. Rocius Trummell, 1881, SANC.
[142] Hertford County Superior Court Minute Docket, Volume 2, 80, SANC.
[143] *State v. William Crockett Reynolds*, Hertford County Civil and Criminal Action
Papers, Box 8, St v Wm Crockett Reynolds, 1893, SANC.

Emanuel Reynolds helped establish and pastored several churches in Hertford County after the Civil War. He married numerous couples in the community including former free people of color and former enslaved people. (Private Collection)

Church of Murfreesboro and also served Mill Neck Baptist Church, New Ahoskie Baptist Church, and Gates County's New Hope Baptist Church. Reynolds pastored New Ahoskie Baptist Church along with Philippi Baptist Church.[144]

Beyond churches, former free people of color were also instrumental in the foundation and operations of several regional religious organizations. After the close of the war, Lemuel Washington Boone helped unify the newly independent Baptist of color in the region under the Roanoke Missionary Baptist Association. As a leader in the association, he represented the interests of Baptist of color in their negotiations with the white establishment in the Baptist church. In 1867, Lemuel Washington Boone assisted in the formation of the Baptist Educational and Missionary Convention of North Carolina. During 1870, Boone, Emanuel Reynolds, and several others from around the state organized the Roanoke Missionary Baptist Relief Association to support ministers working within the Roanoke Missionary Baptist Association. Boone was the association's first president. Through the 1870s, he was a leader in the Sabbath-school movement and served as superintendent of the Eastern North Carolina Sabbath-School Union. Within the Sabbath-School Union, W. D. Newsome acted as assistant superintendent and David D. Weaver held the position of clerk.[145]

Of the many religious organizations founded during the late nineteenth century, the Roanoke Missionary Baptist Association and the West Roanoke Missionary Baptist Association, which broke off from the former organization, were particularly important to the religious and social

---

[144] Meherrin Baptist Church Papers, 1866-1874, nd, Duke University, Rubenstein Library; *Ahoskie Era of Hertford County*, 263, 281; Isaac S. Harrell, "Gates County to 1860," in *Historical Papers of the Trinity College Historical Society* (Durham: Seeman Printer, 1916), 66; "Locals," *Murfreesboro Index*, 30 November 1894; Yvonne Taylor, ed., *Philippi Baptist Church 116th Anniversary* (2002); "New Ahoskie Missionary Baptist Church History," *New Ahoskie Missionary Baptist Church*, accessed May 5, 2016, http://newahoskiebaptistchurch.org/site/cs/aboutus.asp.

[145] J. A. Whitted, *A History of the Negro Baptists of North Carolina* (Raleigh: Edwards and Broughton Printing Company, 1908), 34; Public Laws of the State of North Carolina Passed by the General Assembly; "Eastern North Carolina Sabbath-School Union," *Southern Workman* (October 1875), 87.

Along with several of his siblings, David D. Weaver attended Hampton Institute in Virginia. During Reconstruction, he was an organizer in the local Republican Party and was active in the Sabbath-school movement. He eventually settled in Virginia with his wife Estelle Sprague, granddaughter of the famous abolitionist Frederick Douglass. (State Archives of North Carolina)

lives of Hertford County's former free people of color. Several former free people of color represented their congregations at annual meetings of the Roanoke Missionary Baptist Association and led major reform efforts that joined the Baptist churches with social uplift projects targeted at people of color. David D. Reynolds participated in a meeting as the delegate from Philippi Baptist Church. William C. Jones, the clerk for First Baptist Church of Murfreesboro, represented his congregation. Arrajah Smith, Thomas M. Collins, Joseph B. Catus, and Manassa T. Pope attended meetings on behalf of Pleasant Plains Baptist Church.[146]

In 1886, when churches from Hertford County and other areas joined the newly formed West Roanoke Missionary Baptist Association, former free people of color from Hertford County increased their participation in regional church affairs. William Reid served as moderator of the first meeting while Lemuel Washington Boone's son Isaiah served as corresponding secretary and Joseph B. Catus took the position of secretary. Thomas M. Collins participated in the meeting's opening services. The meeting appointed his brother, John B. Collins, to the standing committee on Sabbath schools while he assisted the standing committee on memorials. Catus and Manassa T. Pope held appointments to the standing committees on temperance and education and helped to revise the organization's constitution. Delegates to the first meeting of the association included John B. Collins and Rufus H. Reynolds of Pleasant Plains Baptist Church, Isaiah Boone and James Starkey Pugh of Philippi Baptist Church, and J. D. Manley of Lincoln Grove Baptist Church.[147]

Pleasant Plains Baptist Church, which free people of color established before the Civil War, continued to flourish during Reconstruction and functioned as an important site for the social and leadership development of the former free people of color and their descendants. In 1870, the church members asserted their independence from the white-controlled

---

[146] *Minutes of the Nineteenth Annual Session of the Roanoke Missionary Baptist Association* (Raleigh: Rev. Caesar Johnson, 1884), 10-12; *Minutes of the Twentieth Annual Session of the Roanoke Missionary Baptist Association* (Raleigh: Baptist Standard Print, 1885), 4, 10, 14-16.

[147] *Organization and Proceedings of the N. C. Western Roanoke Missionary Baptist Association* (Raleigh: Edwards, Broughton and Company, 1886), 1-3, 1-12.

Joseph B. Catus was a leader in politics, education, religion, and social organizations during the late nineteenth and early twentieth centuries. Joseph and his brother William attended Hampton Institute in Virginia. Upon his return to Hertford County, he became active in the Republican Party and served as postmaster in Winton. Catus was also a teacher, trustee of Waters Normal Institute, active member of the Roanoke Missionary Baptist Association, and served as the leader of the Odd Fellows. (Private Collection)

Arrajah Smith was a farmer, storeowner, and longtime secretary of Pleasant Plains Baptist Church. He represented the church at meetings of the Roanoke Missionary Baptist Association. Smith also helped local school districts acquire acreage for public schools. (Private Collection)

Chowan Baptist Association and joined the Roanoke Missionary Baptist Association, a Baptist organization for people of color in eastern North Carolina. With over 400 members by 1885, Pleasant Plains was one of the strongest and most influential congregations in the area. Within the church, former free people of color held numerous leadership posts. During the late nineteenth century, the position of church clerk was essential to the regular workings of the church. Lawrence Weaver, John P. Reynolds, Arrajah Smith, Eff Richard Jones, Lawrence E. Weaver, and Robin Hood Bizzell aided the church in this capacity. James M. Walden, who began serving as church secretary in 1873, maintained the church's financial records. For a short period of time, Thomas M. Collins was the church's interim pastor and became the congregation's first minister of color. The late nineteenth century was also a period of significant organizational development within the church. For example, in 1889, members established the Young Men's Christian Association. The original leaders of the association included Simon P. Collins, president, Joseph B.

James M. Walden was a Civil War veteran and community leader. He was an active member of Pleasant Plains Baptist Church and trustee for Waters Normal Institute. All of Walden's daughters were well-educated for their day and attended schools such as Shaw University and Hampton Institute. He is pictured with his wife Millie Weaver Walden and seven daughters. Seated in the front are Sallie Walden, Lydia Walden, James M. Walden, Millie Weaver Walden, and Cathleen Walden. Standing in the back are Mattie Walden, Georgia Walden, Cora Walden, and Annie Walden. (Private Collection)

Catus, vice president, William H. Smith, secretary, and Eff Richard Jones, treasurer.[148]

---

[148] "Chowan Baptist Association," *Biblical Recorder* (Raleigh), 25 May 1870; *Minutes of the Twentieth Annual Session of Roanoke Missionary Baptist Association* (Raleigh: Baptist Standard Print, 1885), 4, 10, 14-16; M. W. Williams and George W. Watkins, *Who's Who Among North Carolina Negro Baptist: With a Brief History of the Negro Baptist Organizations* (M. W. Williams and George W. Watkins, 1940), 112; Corinne Hare Brummell, *Pleasant Plains Church, 1851-1977* (Ahoskie: Pierce Printers, 1977), 21-22, 50.

Former free people of color used their pre-war educational and wealth advantages to advance education for people of color during Reconstruction. Many worked as teachers including John T. Reynolds, W. D. Newsome, Lawrence E. Weaver, Joseph P. Weaver, Sarah E. Weaver, William W. Jones, Thomas M. Collins, William H. Smith, John W. Jones, Virginia S. Hall, Lavenia Hall, William G. Catus, and Joseph B. Catus. As early as July 1865, John T. Reynolds taught people of color in a school near Murfreesboro. Around the same time, Newsome operated a school that taught both children and adults. After receiving instruction under Newsome, William W. Jones and Lawrence E. Weaver went on to teach their own classes.[149] Newsome participated in the organization of the Freedman's Educational Association of North Carolina and served on its Board of Managers. Newsome and his colleagues sought "to aid in the establishment of schools, from which none shall be excluded on account of color or poverty, and to encourage unsectarian education in this State [North Carolina], especially among the freedmen."[150] During the late 1860s, Newsome and John T. Reynolds rented school buildings at Pleasant Plains and Murfreesboro, respectively, to the Freedmen's Bureau. In later years, several men with significant landholdings such as James M. Walden and Levi Brown provided acreage for schools. In 1885, with the support of several influential whites, the men of color whose freedom pre-dated the Civil War, helped to establish the Winton Colored Academy, later known as Chowan Academy and Waters Normal Institute. This school was the first secondary school for children of color in the county. Levi Brown, Robert A. Reynolds, and Isaiah Boone, all free before the war, were among the original trustees of the school.[151]

Before the establishment of the Winton Colored Academy, people of color only had access to primary school education within the county. Consequently, numerous families and individuals worked and sacrificed to send their children to regional secondary and post-secondary institutions.

---

[149] *Ahoskie Era of Hertford County*, 252-253; Samuel Jordan Wheeler Diary, Volume 2, 80, SHC; William W. Jones Deposition January 10, 1893, Lawrence E. Weaver Pension, Civil War Pensions, NARA.

[150] "Colored Educational Convention," *The Daily Standard* (Raleigh), 11 October 1866.

[151] Hertford County Record of Deeds, Volume N, 569-570, SANC.

Joseph P. Weaver (right) was an educator and political leader in post-Civil War Hertford County. Weaver was one of the first graduates of Hampton Institute in Virginia. He is pictured with his second wife Mattie Reynolds Pope Weaver (left), stepson Jonas Elias Pope, II (center), daughter Cora Weaver (in Mattie's lap), and son Joseph Willis Weaver (in Joseph's lap). (Private Collection)

Hertford County's former free people of color were among the first students to attend some of the region's earliest colleges for people of color including Hampton Institute in Hampton, Virginia and Shaw University in Raleigh, North Carolina. Joseph P. Weaver, son of Willis Weaver and Sally Jones Weaver, was one of the first students to graduate from Hampton Institute. His siblings William B. Weaver, Sarah E. Weaver, and David D. Weaver along with Joseph B. Catus and William G. Catus also attended the school during its earliest days. After their tenures at Hampton Institute, all of these individuals played important roles in the education of people of color. Most noteworthy among these graduates was William B. Weaver, who established a school in Gloucester, Virginia and later with

After his tenure as a student at Hampton Institute, William B. Weaver led the Gloucester Agricultural and Industrial School in Gloucester, Virginia. Later, he and his wife Anna Bolden Weaver founded the Weaver Orphan Home in Hampton, Virginia. (Private Collection)

the assistance of his wife Anna Bolden Weaver operated the Weaver Orphan Home in Hampton.[152]

Shaw University was a popular destination among Hertford County's former free people of color for secondary education. Martha A., Elnora J., and Robert A., children of Andrew and Acre Reynolds, George W., Ophelia L., Alice A., and Walter R., children of Benjamin and Mary Jones Reynolds, William C. and Mary Reid Jones's children John W., Margaret E., and Mary E., along with Antoinette L. Weaver, daughter of Calvin and Annis Weaver, were among the individuals from Murfreesboro's well-to-do families that took classes in Shaw's Classical and Normal Departments. Martha A. and Elnora J. Reynolds were particularly astute students and worked as student teachers while at the university. In 1888, Robert A. Reynolds completed a medical degree to accompany his accomplishments in the Classical department. Marmaduke and Louisa Butler Hall's daughters Virginia S. and Lavenia, Seabird Williamson, the daughter of Eli and Emmaline Hunter Williamson, William Crockett Reynolds, son of Harriett Reynolds, Norman S., son of James and Martha Susan Bizzell Reynolds, James M. and Millie Weaver Walden's daughters Lydia and Cathleen, along with W. H., Willis, and Sarah Jane Keene traveled from the eastern part of Hertford County to attend Shaw and studied in the Classical and Normal Departments. Coming from the same area of the county, Isaiah Boone, son of Lemuel Washington and Charlotte Chavis Boone, took coursework in Shaw's scientific department. Several of the Shaw University students made major impacts in society as educators, business people, and clergy.[153]

---

[152] "The History of the Weaver Family," E. Franklin Frazier Papers Box 131–92, Folder 7; Manuscript Division, Moorland-Spingarn Research Center, Howard University; "Catus Family History," E. Franklin Frazier Papers Box 131–92, Folder 7; Manuscript Division, Moorland-Spingarn Research Center, Howard University; *General Catalogue of the Hampton Normal and Agricultural Institute, Hampton, Virginia, For the Academical Year 1875-6, With a Statement of Its History, Methods and Results* (Hampton: Normal School Steam Press, 1876), 13.

[153] *General Catalogue of the Officers and Students of Shaw University, 1878-1882* (Edward, Broughton, and Company, 1882), 4, 6-9, 13, 16, 18-19; *Catalogue of the Officers and Students of Shaw University, 1883-1884* (Edward, Broughton, and Company, 1884), 8-9, 12; *Catalogue of the Officers and Students of Shaw University,*

Andrew Jackson Archer and Elizabeth Archer were free people of color and married some time before the outbreak of the Civil War. Elizabeth Archer was the daughter of Thomas Archer and Nancy Wiggins Archer. The Archers' marriage was one of several unions between members of the extended Archer family. All of their children who married found spouses from families that were free before 1861. (Private Collection)

*1884-1885* (Edward, Broughton, and Company, 1885), 6, 9-11, 14, 16; *Catalogue of the Officers and Students of Shaw University, 1885-1886* (Edward, Broughton, and Company, 1886), 10, 13, 16; *Catalogue of the Officers and Students of Shaw University, 1887-1888* (Edward, Broughton, and Company, 1888), 11-12.

George Thomas Archer and Mary Mitchell Archer were born free in Hertford County before the Civil War. George Thomas Archer was the son of Thomas Archer and Mildred Smith Archer. In his adult life, he was a trustee of Philippi Baptist Church and an important leader in the Archertown community. Many of the Archers' descendants continue to live in Archertown. (Private Collection)

Martha Sarah Nickens (seated in the center), daughter of William Nickens and Sarah Weaver Nickens, married John Boone (seated to the right), son of Thomas Boone and Eliza Jane Chavis Boone. Both Martha and John came from families that were free before the Civil War. They are pictured here with their children (left to right): Hattie Louvenia Boone, Lula Jane Boone, Thomas Boone, John Quincy Boone, Aaron Boone, and Hersey Sherman Boone. (Private Collection)

Access to political power and greater opportunities for education reshaped the lives of numerous former free people of color, yet in many ways life remained the same in the post-Civil War as before. This was particularly true in regards to the interactions between the former free people of color and the former enslaved people. The former free people of color and the recently emancipated people worked across old social divides in many instances including education and politics. Yet in their day-to-day social lives, especially their familial relationships, the divides of the antebellum period persisted. Former free people of color largely continued to marry and socialize among themselves. Although their weddings did not occur until after the Civil War, when legal marriage to former slaves was possible, none of the children of William and Sarah

Weaver Nickens married into families that were not free before the war. The Nickens children's spouses came from families that shared their pre-war free status such as the Turner, Smith, Britt, Reynolds, Boone, Pierce, Newsome, and Jones families. Thomas Archer's children by Nancy Wiggins Archer and Mildred Smith Archer followed a similar pattern by only marrying members of the Archer, Mitchell, Reynolds, Sears, Flood, Boone, and Lang families. Even when former free people of color had extramarital relationship, their partners often came from families free before the war. After Belvia Sears, who was born free, deserted his wife Margaret Archer, he took up with Julia Ann Melton Smith, a free-born woman. Belvia's sister Melvina, also free-born, married John Hall before living in illicit relationships with Joshua Nickens and Eli Scott, both from free families.[154]

During the post-war nineteenth century, relationships between whites and former free people of color continued to appear among the Hertford County population. Louisiana Weaver, a free woman of color, and James Kiff, a white man developed a relationship that stretched from the pre-Civil War period into the late nineteenth century. Describing his parents' situation, Jesse R. Weaver, the son of the couple explained, "A white man of a good family and a good citizen was the father of mother's children…My father provided a good large farm. One part was hers through his efforts and working the children. He had one farm and house joining our field and he with our help worked both farms. What was made on her farm went to her and what was on his went to him. She raised her own hogs and cattle, and he did likewise. She handled the money she made and he made too." Although many aspects of their lives were separate, Louisiana Weaver, James Kiff, and their family shared experiences just as intimate as many other families. Jesse R. Weaver continued that his father "would come to our house every morning and every night. He would eat there sometimes. He would tell us what to do each day. Ma called him Mr. Kiff and we called him Mr. Kiff. He did

---

[154] Margaret Sears Deposition April 23, 1902, Lawrence Weaver Deposition April 24, 1902, Belvia Sears Pension, Civil War Pensions, NARA; Edwin Sears Deposition March 20, 1925, Joshua Nickens Pension, Civil War Pensions, NARA.

Born into a poor family during the 1830s, Louisiana Weaver, the daughter of Charles Weaver and Delilah Wyatt Weaver, became one of the wealthiest people of color in Hertford County by the time of her death in 1914. She maintained a long-term relationship with James Kiff, a white constable, before marrying Marmaduke Hall. Weaver owned significant property including bonds and real estate. (Private Collection)

Jesse R. Weaver was the son of Louisiana Weaver and James Kiff. He was a rural mail carrier, trustee of Waters Normal Institute, clerk at First Baptist Church of Winton, officer in the Odd Fellows, and secretary of the Benevolent Up-Lift of Eastern North Carolina. (Private Collection)

most of the buying in the home. Ma went for a general shopping about once a year. He arranged for us to have gifts and things as any father would do. I stayed with him mostly till he died. I would stay at nights and sleep with him."[155]

Although the vast majority of former free people of color continued to associate with others who shared similar family backgrounds or with whites, a small number developed relationships with former slaves. At least a few former free women of color married formerly enslaved men who enlisted along with Hertford County's free men of color during the Civil War. While still living in Craven County, where his wartime unit was once based, King Outlaw, a former slave from Bertie County, married Mary Keene, who was born free, in 1869. In 1875, Josephine Reynolds, the free-born daughter of Augustus and Celia Archer Reynolds wed Cado Mountain, who was born enslaved in Bertie County and was a veteran of the war. William B. Weaver, who was born free, married Anna Bolden, a former slave and fellow attendee of Hampton Institute.[156]

In many ways, the situation for Hertford County's former free people of color and their descendants at the end of the nineteenth century had improved tremendously since the outbreak and suppression of the Confederate rebellion. Yet radical white politicians and thugs threatened those historic gains. During the post-Civil War years, former free people of color made inroads in politics, business, religion, and education. This was especially true for those individuals who had brought skills, education, and wealth from the pre-Civil War period into the new era. Nevertheless, from the beginning of Reconstruction, white conservatives targeted the former free people of color along with recently emancipated people in an effort to regain power from the Republican Party and

---

[155] "The Weaver Brothers Family," E. Franklin Frazier Papers Box 131–92, Folder 7; Manuscript Division, Moorland-Spingarn Research Center, Howard University.
[156] King Outlaw Deposition February 11, 1891, Martha J. Jones Affidavit June 13, 1899, King Outlaw Pension, Civil War Pensions, NARA; John A. Northcott Deposition December 10, 1910, Cado Mountain Pension, Civil War Pensions, NARA; Record for Cado Mountain, Registers of Signatures of Depositors in Branches of the Freedman's Savings and Trust Company, 1865-1875, M816, NARA; "Family History of Mrs William Weaver," E. Franklin Frazier Papers Box 131–92, Folder 7; Manuscript Division, Moorland-Spingarn Research Center, Howard University.

reinstitute an alternative version of the pre-emancipation social order. They sought a world dominated by conservative ideals and principles, a society that was separate and unequal.

# Chapter 4:
# Jim Crow

During most of the twentieth century, the politics and customs of Jim Crow shaped life for the people of Hertford County. The former free people of color and their descendants were no exception, and rather quickly, they learned to adapt to this unprecedented situation. At the beginning of the century, they along with others of their station across the southern U.S. saw their political privileges largely disappear. They would have to wait decades to regain any semblance of formal political power. The elites among them had to develop their authority and create opportunity within segregated colored spaces. Within schools, businesses, and churches, they cultivated positions of influence. Jim Crow was a burden for all people of color, yet it did not completely denigrate the position of the former free people of color and their descendants.

As the first years of the twentieth century passed, the descendants of free people of color saw their place in the formal operations of their county dwindle. Although people of color were the majority in Hertford County, activities at the state level quickly diminished their influence on formal politics. A 1900 state constitutional amendment required voters to be able to read and write a portion of the North Carolina constitution and pay a poll tax. In addition, legislators added to the amendment a "grandfather clause," which made an exception for potential voters who voted or had an ancestor who voted before January 1, 1867. The 1867 voter requirement allowed most white people to vote and helped to exclude most people of color from the polls, since North Carolina had yet to enfranchise the former slaves before this date. In Hertford County, many of the former free people of color and their descendants registered during the first decade of the 1900s. Nevertheless, their registration and vote without the support of the former slaves and their descendants largely kept all candidates of color and their white Republican allies out of office.

Whites' enforcement of other Jim Crow policies and customs pushed the former free people of color and their descendants into segregated social circles and spaces. Regardless of the color of their skin, whites required all people of color to deal with second-rate colored accommodations. Since the end of the Civil War, they had attended segregated colored schools, and by the first decades of the century, whites created segregated white and colored seating in places such as theaters while certain public places had separate entrances for whites and people of color. Hertford County citizens kept separate white and colored social organizations including churches, fraternal groups, and clubs. Semi-open familial relationships between men and women of different racial categories largely disappeared. Up to the end of legal segregation, the local newspaper regularly segregated the news related to people of color from the rest of the stories in the "Colored News" or "Negro News" sections. On some occasions, the *Hertford County Herald* followed the practice of referring to people of color as "Aunt" or "Uncle" instead of "Mister," "Missus," or "Miss." A March 19, 1915 article in the paper gave Mary Nickens the title of "Aunt" while it listed the white women in the same section as "Mrs."[157]

Although the minority in Hertford County, whites created a mythical image of the county in which they were at its core. They depicted their spaces and organizations as the mainstream while always defining the events and societies connected to the majority of the population as simply "Negro" or "Colored" gatherings and groups. Some whites placed a statue in front of the county courthouse memorializing the white men who served the Confederacy and fought for the preservation of slavery while the contributions of the men of color who helped preserve the Union and helped defeat the pro-slavery cause received no public monument or mention. Their versions of history always placed whites at the center and made them the primary focus, whether in the form of the more conservative Benjamin B. Winborne's *The Colonial and State Political History of Hertford County, North Carolina*, which disparaged the contributions of Reconstruction-period leaders W. D. Newsome and

---

[157] "Winton Waveletts," *Hertford County Herald*, 19 March 1915.

William Reid, or *The Ahoskie Era of Hertford County*, a publication that included memorials to the county's people of color.[158]

Whites through their discriminatory actions continued to remind people of Jim Crow's actual purposes, to keep certain whites in power and to provide other whites with privileges that would convince them to preserve that power structure. The whites with political control in the county operated in similar ways to their other southern peers. They provided white schools with disproportionate funding and paid their teachers more than teachers of color. A 1911 report revealed that Hertford County spent $3,076 on its colored schools compared to the $5,146 allocated to the white schools. Yet 1,311 pupils attended the colored schools while only 754 students went to the schools for whites. Although the 33 teachers at the colored schools were responsible for more pupils per teacher than the 32 instructors at the white schools, the county paid teachers at the colored schools $25 per month and those at the white schools $30 per month. The county did not have a public high school for people of color until the 1920s when the county established Hertford County Training School and took over Waters Normal Institute, which became Waters Training School. Furthermore, the officials refused to allocate public funding to support school buses for children of color.[159]

Discrimination against people of color was not confined to the public sector as even private white organizations sought to reaffirm white supremacy. The Ku Klux Klan, a white supremacist organization, was active in the area. In 1947, the white-run Kiwanis in Hertford County made national headlines for preventing Harvey Jones, a descendant of free people of color, from claiming a Cadillac that he won in a raffle sponsored by the group. The organization partly capitulated after national outrage

---

[158] Benjamin B. Winborne, *The Colonial and State Political History of Hertford County, North Carolina* (Raleigh: Edwards and Broughton, 1906); *The Ahoskie Era of Hertford County* (Ahoskie: Parker Brothers, 1939).

[159] W. E. Burghardt DuBois and Augustus Granville Dill, ed., *The Common School and the Negro American* (Atlanta: Atlanta University Press, 1911), 46; *Ahoskie Era of Hertford County*, 55-56, 69.

In 1947, the Kiwanis Club in Hertford County prevented Harvey Jones from claiming a Cadillac, which he won in a raffle sponsored by the organization, because he was a person of color. After national outrage, the Kiwanis gave Jones a check for the value of the Cadillac. Harvey Jones (right) with his check in hand is pictured with his father Starkey Jones (left). This ACME photograph appeared in newspapers across the country. (Private Collection)

and awarded Jones a cash prize.[160] On rare but noteworthy occasions, whites sought to demonstrate their alleged superiority through violence. At a 1943 court term, Judge W. H. S. Burgwyn sentenced Chester "Chet" Rogerson, a white man, after his conviction for the murder of John "Bud" Keene, a descendant of free people of color. Rogerson killed the deceased because Keene supposedly called him a "foul name." According to the sheriff, Rogerson explained, "no nigger is going to call me that."[161]

White policymakers designed Jim Crow laws and rules under the assumption that people could be easily divided into two groups, colored and white. Yet the social patterns that developed before the Jim Crow period prevented this supposition from becoming a full reality. Through the first half of the twentieth century, many descendants continued to follow the social patterns of their free ancestors, especially in marriage. Many descendants also continued to socialize with others of the same background. Although people in Hertford County labeled the descendants of the free people of color and the children, grandchildren, and great grandchildren of the enslaved people as "negroes" or "colored people," common categorization did not reflect social congruency, particularly during the early part of the century. During a visit to the Archertown neighborhood in 1930, the sociologist E. Franklin Frazier made the following observations: "Archertown is a settlement of about twenty families on 2500 acres of land. The inhabitants are mulattoes, many of whom have blond hair and blue eyes…Among the families in Archertown there is considerable intermarriage between cousins…The school in the community has always been taught by mulatto teachers. They do not mix much with the darker members of the community except as they might meet at the Sunday School Convention."[162] The situation in Archertown was an extreme example, but many of the practices described by Frazier applied to other descendants of free people of color during the early

---

[160] "Klan Rally Wednesday Night Nets $152; Sheriff's Men, Gov. Moore Attacked," *Hertford County Herald*, 6 August 1965; "Jones Gets Cash Instead of Auto," *The Pittsburgh Courier*, 2 August 1947.

[161] "Whites Sentence For Killing Negro," *Norfolk Journal and Guide*, 6 March 1943.

[162] "Archertown," E. Franklin Frazier Papers Box 131-92, Folder 7; Manuscript Division, Moorland-Spingarn Research Center, Howard University.

twentieth century. Concepts of "black community" or "race solidarity" did not fit into their worldview; community was not based in race but in familial connections and a shared past.

During the first decade of the 1900s, many descendants of free people of color held a higher political status than their other non-white peers because of their ancestry. This situation reinforced perceived difference between the descendants of free people of color and those of the enslaved population. In 1900, North Carolina passed the grandfather clause as part of a constitutional amendment, stating that only men who were voters before January 1, 1867 or whose ancestors were voters before this date could register to vote. By default, most descendants of slaves could not vote under the grandfather clause because their forebears would have ineligible for the franchise before 1867. Many free men of color, however, could vote at some point before that time. As a result descendants of many of the old free families of color including the Boone, Weaver, Nickens, Flood, Garnes, Jones, Hall, Wiggins, Bizzell, Chavis, Melton, Smothers, Smith, Reid, Pierce, Pugh, and Reynolds families registered to vote during the era of the grandfather clause. Many non-white voters named free men of color such as Anderson Melton, William Nickens, Augustus Reynolds, Daniel Garnes, Jesse Keene, Dempsey Flood, William Smothers, John Bizzell, William Hall, Starkey Pugh, Jordan Pierce, Jacob Smith, Elvey Lewis, Edward Wiggins, Harry Chavis, Jerry Reid, Allen Hall, and Charles Weaver as their ancestors who could vote before 1867. Between 1902 and 1908, at least 134 individuals descended from free people of color registered to vote in Hertford County. Many other counties followed the same path as Hertford County and allowed those individuals descended from free persons of color to register to participate in elections.

In a few cases, descendants of the free people of color registered to vote through their descent from their white progenitors instead of their free non-white ancestors. Preston Hall and his nephew William James Hall both claimed their right to vote through their white forefather Thomas Winborne. These men likely named Winborne as their ancestor because they had no non-white male ancestors who had voted in recent memory. William James Hall's father, Albert G. Vann, and his mother's father,

Dudley "Erk" Weaver (top left), Patrick Henry Pierce (top center), John Pat Jones (top right), Albert Hall (bottom left), Preston Hunter (bottom center), and Nathaniel T. Lang (bottom right) registered to vote as descendants of their grandfathers. Weaver claimed descent from Charles Weaver. Pierce registered as a descendant of Allen Hall. Jones named William Jones as his ancestor who could vote before 1867. When registering, Hall gave the name of William Hall. Hunter provided the name of Willis Weaver in order to register. The voter record for Lang gives the name of his grandfather Jordan Pierce. (Private Collections)

When they registered to vote, Willis E. Jones (top left), John Robert Chavis (top center), Burnell Wiggins (top right), Frederick Douglass Robbins (bottom left), John E. Lewis (bottom center), and William H. Collins (bottom right) claimed descent from ancestors born during the late 1700s and early 1800s. Jones named his grandfather William Jones as his ancestor. John Robert Chavis was one of several men who registered to vote as descendants of Harry Chavis, his great grandfather. Wiggins provided the name of William Nickens. Robbins registered as a descendant of his grandfather Augustus Reynolds. When registering, Lewis gave the name of Jacob Smith, his mother's father. John Bizzell, Collins's grandfather, is listed as his ancestor in the voter register. (Private Collections)

Several members of the Hall family including William James Hall (left) and his sons
Crawleigh Finney Hall (center) and Wells Hall (right) registered to vote under the
"Grandfather Clause" by claiming descent from their ancestor Thomas "Tom"
Winborne. (Private Collection)

Winborne, were white, leaving him with no non-white father or
grandfather.[163]

In many instances, descendants of free people of color found ways to
disassociate themselves from the "colored" or "negro" labels used by
whites to deny them certain privileges. In 1939, the family of Abram
Thomas Archer and Martha Wiggins Archer won a court case that made
them legally "white" and protected them from the discrimination faced by
people of color. The court declared, "That the petitioners are white people,
not being descended from any person of Negro blood within three
generations inclusive, that the ancestors of the petitioners trace back their
blood on the paternal side through white men to Revolutionary times; that
Martha A. Archer, wife of A. T. Archer, was the daughter of Barthemus
Wiggins who was a Confederate soldier and fought under General J. E. B.
Stuart." Furthermore, the judgment explained, "That the petitioners and

[163] Hertford County, Secretary of State Voter Registration Records, 1902-1908, SANC.
See Secretary of State Voter Registration Records for other counties for addition
examples of voters descended from free people of color.

their families do not associate with Negroes and never have done so; that the petitioners are not generally treated as white people but are wrongfully excluded from association with the white race."[164] Many others, however, did not seek court rulings; instead they simply left Hertford County and moved to places where their family history was unknown. Through this method, they avoided categorization as "colored" or "negro" and removed themselves from the associations and segregated positions required by law and custom for "colored" people. Joshua Nickens was one of many people considered "colored" in Hertford County, who by leaving the area, became accepted in their new community as "white." After his death in 1924, Bessie Gilligan Nickens, an Irish woman and Joshua's last wife, declared that had she known he was a "colored" man, "I would not have married him."[165]

Beyond promoting white supremacy, Jim Crow segregation slowly, but effectively chopped away at the social distance that many former free people of color and their descendants attempted to keep between themselves and other people of color. The marriage patterns established by their ancestors largely stayed intact during the first half of the century. Yet sharing Jim Crow spaces with the descendants of former slaves eventually led to greater intermarriage and more interaction in general. During the Jim Crow period, the descendants of both free people of color and enslaved people attended the same schools for many years, which created a level of familiarity among people that had not existed during the slavery period or Reconstruction. Calvin Scott Brown, the son of former slaves and the rector of Waters Normal Institute, took direct action to breakdown the divisions of the past. Against the protest of parents, Brown purposely mixed up the children from different backgrounds.[166] The work of Brown

---

[164] "Archer Family Officially Becomes Members White Race," *Hertford County Herald*, 28 September 1939. Bartemus Wiggins mentioned in the article served in the Confederate forces as a musician not a soldier according to his Confederate Service Record. See *Compiled Service Records of Confederate Soldiers Who Served in Organizations from the State of North Carolina*, M270, NARA.

[165] Bessie Nickens Deposition January 31, 1925, Joshua Nickens Pension, Civil War Pensions, NARA.

[166] "Document Furnished By Dr. C. S. B.," E. Franklin Frazier Papers Box 131–92, Folder 7; Manuscript Division, Moorland-Spingarn Research Center, Howard University.

Norman Hall (left) and Tearsie L. Simmons (right) were trustees of Waters Normal Institute during the 1920s. Norman Hall was one of the most successful people of color in Hertford County during the early twentieth century. He was also a leader in the Masons. Upon his death in 1927, Hall owned real estate, stocks, and bonds. He donated a significant part of his estate to Pleasant Plains Baptist Church. Tearsie L. Simmons was a farm owner and trustee of Philippi Baptist Church. He was also one of many men who claimed the right to vote during period of the "Grandfather Clause." Tearsie registered to vote as a descendant of his grandfather Starkey Pugh. (Private Collections)

and others created an environment in which the descendants of free people of color and slaves crossed social boundaries for common purposes.

Although Jim Crow policies limited the opportunities of the descendants of the free people of color, they found multiple ways to create a rich social life and often found leadership opportunities within that social world. Schools were one of their key institutions for socialization and leadership development, and several important social organizations for adults developed around the county's schools. The establishment of Winton Colored Academy included the foundation of the Chowan Educational Association, which helped to raise funds for the school. Former free people of color and their descendants such as Joseph B. Catus and James M. Walden participated in this organization. The school's

107

Board of Trustees also provided men of this background with leadership opportunities. Norman Hall, William James Hall, Norman Lassiter, Tearsie L. Simmons, William Reid, and Jesse R. Weaver, all descendants of free people of color, served on the school's board of trustees during the 1920s. The most significant leadership roles that the schools provided were the positions held by administrators and teachers. Numerous descendants of Hertford County's free people of color served the schools in these capacities. Among this number were Addie Hall Lawrence, the county's first Jeanes supervisor in charge of improving the rural schools, Addie Collins and Ardelle Garrett, principals at the Pleasant Plains School, Gladys Reid Lawrence, principal at the Vaughntown School, and Henry D. Cooper, the principal of Ahoskie Graded School (R. L. Vann High School). Many parents asserted their leadership capabilities through the schools' parent-teacher associations. In 1950, the leadership of the C. S. Brown High School PTA was composed entirely of descendants of free people of color. The officers of the organization included Arthur H. Brett, president, Lemuel M. Manley, vice president, Bessie Keene Hall, secretary, Myrtle Hall Smith, assistant secretary, and Alice Jones Scott, treasurer.[167]

Schools, of course, were important sites of socialization and development for young people. The schools offered the youth a variety of activities including sports, singing, and community service. In the early twentieth century, students at Waters Normal Institute enjoyed playing sports such as tennis, basketball, and baseball. Later, football became a popular pastime for youth at C. S. Brown and R. L. Vann Schools. Students at other schools also participated in these activities. Several student groups and clubs provided students with a social outlet. For example, the Glee Club was popular among students at Ahoskie Graded School and Waters Training School. Club members performed in concerts and contests in Hertford County and around the region. Students

---

[167] *Ahoskie Era of Hertford County*, 254-255, 267; "Winton," *Norfolk Journal and Guide*, 23 April 1927; "Personally Speaking," *Hertford County Herald*, 9 August 1945; "Harrellsville Community Fair Marked Successful Event," *Hertford County Herald*, 29 October 1936; "Brown School PTA Elects New Officers," *Hertford County Herald*, 28 September 1950.

Addie Hall Lawrence, a graduate of Shaw University and daughter of Marmaduke Hall and Louisa Butler Hall, taught at several schools and served as the community's first Jeanes supervisor. She was also active in many community organizations including the Ahoskie Home Demonstration Club and the Missionary Circle at New Ahoskie Baptist Church. (Private Collection)

Gladys Reid Lawrence was a principal at the Vaughntown School during the twentieth century. She was the granddaughter of the political and religious leader William Reid. (Private Collection)

Teachers Georgia Hall Weaver (standing left of Elouise K. Pierce) and Elouise K. Pierce (seated left) accompanied students from Robert L. Vann High School on the annual Washington, DC trip. On this particular trip in 1953, students met with First Lady Mamie Eisenhower (seated right) in the White House rose garden. (Private Collection)

throughout the county were active in the 4-H Club based out of the schools. During the 1930s, 4-H members participated in various projects such as gardening, farming, raising animals, canning, sewing, and learning about health and nutrition. The New Homemakers of America (NHA) and Home Economic Clubs played important roles in the social lives of many school-aged girls. Georgia Hall Weaver was the sponsor of the NHA at R. L. Vann during the mid-century. Under her guidance, young ladies and men traveled beyond the limits of Hertford County to places such as Washington, DC to learn about the world beyond their little rural community. The local schools also hosted chapters of the New Farmers of America (NFA), a young men's organization. John Manley gained a brief spotlight while a member of the C. S. Brown NFA. In 1943, he won a district quiz contest on Negro life and advanced to a state contest held in Greensboro. The chapter at R. L. Vann promoted the successes of many youth including Wallace James, who won awards from the Vann Club for being the top NFA corn grower and prizes at the NFA national convention for repair and mechanics during the 1940s and 1950s.[168]

White officials' unwillingness to fund the county's public colored school system at the same rate as those for white people forced administrators, teachers, students, and parents of color to organize and lead their own fundraising campaigns to support their educational infrastructure. Administrators worked tirelessly to raise funds for their schools. In 1951, H. D. Cooper, as principal of R. L. Vann High School, started a collection to purchase instruments for students in the band and to pay the band director. Teachers organized numerous efforts to keep their schools afloat. Under the leadership of teachers Ardelle Garrett, Bessie Keene Hall, and Viola Hall, the Pleasant Plains School held a Friday night program to support the beautification of the school building during the fall of 1927. The program events included games for the children and a marching contest in which Annie Mary Reynolds and Dewey Keene took home the winning prize. Fannie Reynolds Sawyer and Dicie Hall, teachers at the Walden School, hosted a baby contest fundraiser at the school in 1937. Willis Jacobia Jones, Edward Carol Boone, and Ella Mae Simmons were the prize-winning babies in the competition.[169]

Parents took on numerous projects in order to improve the school experiences of children deprived by white officials of the proper funding for their schools. In the early 1940s, the Pleasant Plains School PTA sponsored a library for their children. During the same period, Ardelle Garrett, the school principal, headed a joint effort with the Pleasant Plains School PTA, Pleasant Plains Baptist Church, the Works Progress Administration, and the Pleasant Plains community to construct a

---

[168] "Ahoskie Glee Club Sing Christmas Carols," *Norfolk Journal and Guide*, 28 December 1940; "Ahoskie Wins Top Honors In Contest," *Norfolk Journal and Guide*, 26 April 1941; "Fine Projects by Negro 4-H Clubs," *Hertford County Herald*, 1 July 1937; "Wins Contest," *Hertford County Herald*, 4 March 1943; "R. L. Vann Girls Make Three-Day Trip to Washington, D. C.," *Hertford County Herald*, 1 June 1950; "Student Places," *Hertford County Herald*, 15 April 1943; "Wallace James Gets National NFA Honors," *Hertford County Herald*, 26 October 1950; "Wallace James and Floyd Reid Named Top Corn Growers," *Hertford County Herald*, 30 November 1950.
[169] "Ahoskie, N. C.," *Norfolk Journal and Guide*, 10 December 1927; "Much Interest," *Hertford County Herald*, 16 December 1937.

Ardelle Garrett was a longtime principal and teacher at the Pleasant Plains School. During her tenure, Garrett spearheaded several efforts to fundraise for and improve the school and the larger community. One of her most noteworthy successes was the construction of a playground at the school. In addition to her education work, Garrett served as president of the Hertford County Council of Home Demonstration Clubs and the State Council of Home Demonstration Clubs of North Carolina. She was also active in a number of important community organizations including Pleasant Plains Baptist Church, the Baptist Young People's Union, and the Ever Ready Art Club. Later in life, Garrett married Pierce Boone. (Private Collection)

Arthur H. Brett was a deacon and clerk and Julia Pierce Brett was a deaconess at Pleasant Plains Baptist Church. Arthur H. Brett was also a successful farmer and president of the C. S. Brown High School PTA. As PTA president, he helped to secure much-needed equipment for students at the school. (Private Collection)

playground adjacent to the school. A reporter for the local newspaper described the playground as "probably the cleanest, most attractive spot in Hertford County."[170] H. D. Cooper's band fundraiser took place with the assistance of R. L. Vann's PTA. The C. S. Brown PTA under the leadership of Arthur H. Brett and Bessie Keene Hall led a fundraiser for the purchase of a new bus. The efforts of the PTA along with assistance from the students and larger community allowed the school to purchase the all-steel body bus in 1951. The school acquired the bus so that youth involved in sports such as football, baseball, and basketball or organizations like the Glee Club could attend activities away from the C. S. Brown campus. Before the purchase, students depended on privately owned vehicles to transport them to games and other events.[171]

---

[170] "Pleasant Plains," *Hertford County Herald*, 30 July 1942.
[171] "$2,314 Collected in Band Fund At R. L. Vann School Since March," *Hertford County Herald*, 8 November 1951; "Negro Children, Parents Pitch in to Purchase 'Brand

Religious institutions also played a key role in the social lives and leadership development of descendants of free people of color during the Jim Crow period. Pleasant Plains Baptist Church, which their ancestors organized in the mid-nineteenth century, along with Philippi Baptist Church, Newsome Grove Baptist Church, and First Baptist Church of Winton (also known as South Winton) had significant numbers of parishioners of this background. Other local churches also had them among their congregations. Descendants served as deacons, deaconesses, and trustees of these institutions, and they participated in the churches' choirs and missionary organizations. Pleasant Plains Baptist Church had an active Baptist Young People's Union (BYPU) during the 1920s. The BYPU was an educational and missionary association. In 1926, Solomon Keene presided over the organization. Under his leadership, the group hosted a service at the church with talks given by Ardelle Garrett, Rufus H. Reynolds, and Samuel F. Lewis. The Missionary Circle at New Ahoskie Baptist Church also produced public programming. During July 1930, the group organized a program under the direction of Addie Hall Lawrence and Gabrilla Branson Garnes. Their event included paper presentations along with choir and solo music. In addition, vacation bible school provided youth with instruction and play time. In 1937, 78 children between ages three and 15 participated in vacation bible school at Pleasant Plains Baptist Church. The attendees received lessons from the bible in addition to enjoying time dedicated to art, music, and games. At the end of the term, the children presented their artwork, music, and biblical expertise. They also staged a one-act play under the direction of their instructor Thelma Ruth Brett.[172]

Following the path set by their ancestors in the late nineteenth century, descendants continued to participate in regional religious organizations and gatherings. These associations and events provided

New' All-Steel Body Bus for C. S. Brown High School of Winton," *Hertford County Herald*, 21 June 1951.

[172] *Philippi Baptist Church 116th Anniversary* (2002); "Ahoskie, N. C.," *Norfolk Journal and Guide*, 7 August 1926; Hertford County Record of Deeds, Volume 65, 436, SANC; "Ahoskie, N. C.," *Norfolk Journal and Guide*, 12 July 1930; "Vacation Bible School Pleasant Plains Church," *Hertford County Herald*, 19 August 1937.

them with opportunity to build networks and develop social uplift projects. Into the twentieth century, meetings of the West Roanoke Missionary Baptist Association allowed them the opportunity to fulfill their religious and social agendas. Descendants of free people of color represented the congregations at Pleasant Plains, Newsome Grove, First Baptist Church of Winton, and Philippi. The association supported numerous programs and institutions including Waters Normal Institute. Although men originally dominated the West Roanoke Missionary Baptist Association, by the late 1890s women began to assert a role in the organization through the Woman's Home and Foreign Mission Union. During the early twentieth century, Esther Boone and Addie Hall Lawrence served as presidents of the women's organization. Fannie Jones Hare, Nancy Ella Hall Reid, and Texanna Jones Jenkins also were active in the union.[173]

Numerous fraternal organizations and clubs satisfied the social needs of the descendants of Hertford County's free people of color during the Jim Crow decades. Throughout the twentieth century, descendants participated in the Masons, Odd Fellows, Eastern Stars, and Elks. Joseph B. Catus served as the Grand Master of the Odd Fellows during the first decade of the century. Several descendants held leadership roles with the Masonic lodges in Hertford County. In 1925, George Hall, Efton Reid, Robin H. Bizzell, William Norman Brown, Nathaniel T. Lang, and Melton Lassiter, all descendants of the free people of color, were officers in the Union Lodge. Descendants Samuel T. Collins, Arthur H. Brett, Hiram B. Weaver, William James Hall, Percy Carol Weaver, Abner J. Melton, John Lewis, and James C. Weaver were officers of the Perfect Ashlar Lodge in Winton during the same year. In 1945, Solomon Keene of the Union Lodge was Grand Orator for all of the Masons in North Carolina. During the 1930s, the Benevolent Up-Lift of Eastern North Carolina operated in

---

[173] *Minutes of the Twenty-Fifth Annual Session of the West Roanoke Association Held with Cedar Landing Baptist Church in Bertie County, N. C.* (Wilson: Barrett's Print, 1910), 10-11, 17-19; *Minutes of the Twenty-Seventh Annual Session of West Roanoke Association, Held with Sandy Branch Baptist Church, near Roxobel, Bertie Co.* (Goldsboro: Nash Brothers, 1913), 11-15, 19; *Minutes of the Woman's Home and Foreign Mission Union of the West Roanoke Association Held with the Circle of First Baptist Church Powellsville Bertie County, N. C.* (1927), 1-5.

James Cornelius Weaver (left), son of Sarah Eliza Weaver, and Samuel T. Collins (right), son of John B. Collins and Georgiana Artis Collins, were active in the Masons during the 1920s. Both men were also avid outdoorsmen. Collins was best known as an embalmer for Hertford County Undertakers. (Private Collection)

Hertford County. Descendants Samuel T. Collins and Jesse R. Weaver were members of this burial organization. The Ambassadors Club was another important organization for the leading men of color in the area, and several descendants participated in this organization including Joseph D. Weaver as president, Sherman P. Hall, vice president, Julius A. Watford, business manager, and William Hall, chairman of recreation.[174]

Women's organizations enabled descendants of free people of color to maintain active social lives and take on leadership roles otherwise unavailable to women throughout the Jim Crow period. A small number of women participated in the Ever Ready Art Club during the 1920s. Members of the club included Daffie Weaver Boone, Dessie Chavis, Ardelle Garrett, Julia Bizzelle Watford, Donie Weaver Hall, Bessie Keene Hall, Sarah Hamilton Reynolds, Annie Hall, and Mary Lewis. In the 1930s, Sallie Y. Bizzelle led the Garden and Poultry Club, which sponsored an exhibit booth at the Atlantic District Fair. In the late 1940s, several women organized the Lady Ambassadors Club, a social and civic organization. Most of the club's members were descendants of free people of color and usually the wives of successful businessmen in the county. They hosted events such as carnivals and formal dances in Ahoskie. The Polly Anna Club operated during the same period and helped raise money for local charity cases. On April 10, 1951, the club announced its annual talent exhibit. The club members directed the funds accrued from such events to the less fortunate.[175]

---

[174] "Complimentary Reception, *New Berne Weekly Journal*, 23 October 1906; C. S. Brown, *Proceedings of the Fifty-fifth Communication of the Most Worshipful Grand Lodge F. A. A. M* (Durham: Seeman Printery Incorporated, 1926), 90 132; "Attending Meeting," *Hertford County Herald*, 18 October 1945; "Colored News," *Hertford County Herald*, 10 February 1938; "Officers and Members of the Ambassadors Club of Ahoskie, N. C.," *Norfolk Journal and Guide*, 12 February 1949.

[175] "Ahoskie, N. C.," *Norfolk Journal and Guide*, 10 December 1927; "Garden and Poultry Club Plan for Exhibit," *Hertford County Herald*, 29 September 1938; "Polly Anna Club Gives Charity Program," *Norfolk Journal and Guide*, 27 June 1953; "Club to Present Show Tuesday," *Hertford County Herald*, 10 April 1951; "Inaugurated 'Lady Ambassadors' At Recent Dance in Ahoskie, N. C.," *Norfolk Journal and Guide*, 12 February 1949; "Lady Ambassadors Sponsor Carnival In Ahoskie," *Norfolk Journal and Guide*, 23 October 1948; Evelyn Mansfield Swann, "National Social Whirl," *Norfolk Journal and Guide*, 28 February 1953.

Sallie Y. Bizzelle was a longtime teacher at Waters Normal Institute (later C. S. Brown School). She led the Garden and Poultry Club, which sponsored an exhibit booth at the Atlantic District Fair. (Private Collection)

The Polly Anna Club held numerous fundraisers to support local charity cases. In the front row (left to right) are Aurie Keene, Annie Watford Simmons, Lala Wilson Gatling, and Aberdeen Clanton Watford. Dora Jones Porter, Carrie Jones, Vertley Nickens Jones, Olga Jones Reid, Elenora Stephenson Chavis, Eunice Downing Manley, and Viola Hall Chavis are in the second row (left to right). In the third row (left to right) are Agnes Hall Weaver, Alice Jones Nickens, Theora Mitchell Stallings, Albina Sears Hall, Elizabeth Manley Hall, Effie Jones Gadsden, Thelma Susan Jones Hall, Timie Collins Weaver, and Lillian Royster Weaver. Doris Joyner Reynolds, Susan Reynolds Brown, Dicie Hall Reid, and Melba Ashe Chavis are in the back row (left to right). (Private Collection)

The Hertford County Home Demonstration Club and its local branches served the needs of many women as organizations focused on neighborhood issues, gardening, and home life. As part of their work, the local clubs held large public events. On September 28, 1945, the various local clubs sponsored an achievement day hosted by the Pleasant Plains Home Demonstration Club. Achievement Day events included a clothing demonstration, dress review and competition, exhibits of canned meats and vegetables, a poster display, and a table of sugarless desserts. The local clubs also hosted numerous lectures and small demonstrations. In 1950, the Cofield Home Demonstration Club, under Nellie Gray Manley Melton's leadership, held a meeting at Jimmie Combo's house that included a discussion titled "Family Life." On August 17, 1950, the president of the Pleasant Plains Home Demonstration Club, Bessie Keene Hall, demonstrated how to make better cornbread. At a meeting in 1956, the group listened to a talk delivered by Cora Hunter Chavis titled "How Do You Score as a Good Neighbor."[176]

By the early 1960s, community uplift became a major focus of people across Hertford County including many descendants of free people of color. Through a variety of organizations, they developed programs to beautify their neighborhoods and fight poverty. Sally Eaton Jones joined her neighbors in Winton, both of color and white, in planning to improve their town. The group's project proposals included cleaning cemeteries and vacant lots and demolishing buildings that were in disrepair. Under Jimmie Combo's leadership, the Cofield Community Development Association participated in several community improvement projects. In 1963, the association focused on several important initiatives within Cofield. Jimmie Combo and James C. Smith joined with children in Cofield to renovate the community playground. Smith and Tupper W. Jones worked on a project to install signs around the community while several members of the association helped procure new lights for the street

[176] "Achievement Day For Negro HD Clubs," *Hertford County Herald*, 4 October 1945; "Cofield Club Hears Report On Meeting," *Hertford County Herald*, 3 May 1951; "Cofield Club Holds Meeting," *Hertford County Herald*, 9 March 1950; "Pleasant Plains Club Has Meeting," *Hertford County Herald*, 22 August 1950.

During the 1960s, Jimmie Combo led the Cofield Community Development Association. The association participated in a variety of community projects including infrastructure improvements and anti-poverty efforts. Combo was also an active member of the Cofield Home Demonstration Club. (Private Collection)

and playground. That same year, the group also sponsored a family garden tour. By 1965, the association began to take serious steps to fight poverty within the community, and the group agreed to assist with the Hertford County Economic Development Committee's pilot anti-poverty project.[177]

In 1920, people of color in Hertford County organized the Atlantic District Fair, which served a variety of leadership and social purposes. Within the Jim Crow social order, the Atlantic District Fair was supposed to be the fair for "Negroes." Numerous descendants of free people of color held leadership roles in the fair including Clarence Chavis, who acted as the fair's president starting in 1937, and J. Eley Reid, who was treasurer and manager of the fair. Attendees of the fair enjoyed a number of attractions including exhibits, fireworks, and racing. Although members of the community considered the Atlantic District Fair a "Negro" event, both people of color and whites enjoyed the fair, especially the races. Aside from these activities, the fair also provided people of color with a space to display their talents. In 1950, the fair hosted the first swine show and sale. Talmadge Chavis's entry of a Spotted Poland China took the top spot in the junior sows category while Jim Chavis and Cling L. Pierce also had grand champion submissions. At that same fair, Claudia Hare Chavis demonstrated her acumen in the culinary arts. She captured at least 19 prizes in can goods competition, and all of her submissions won awards. After establishing her dominance at the local fair, she traveled to the State Fair in Raleigh and secured 9 different first and second place ribbons. That same year, for the second time, she won the county-wide food contest.[178]

---

[177] "Eure Thinks 'New Winton' Idea Would Help Town," *Hertford County Herald*, 5 November 1963; "Cofield Community Work Supported By Group Action," *Hertford County Herald*, 18 June 1963; "Cofield Community Group Told of Recreation Needs," *Hertford County Herald*, 6 August 1963; "Family Garden Tour At Cofield Had 32 Stops," *Hertford County Herald*, 2 July 1963; "Cofield Organizes For Anti-Poverty Planning," *Hertford County Herald*, 26 March 1965.

[178] "Negro Fair Will Be Held October," *Hertford County Herald*, 24 September 1936; "Scenes at Atlantic District Fair Last Week," *Norfolk Journal and Guide*, 23 October 1937; "First Swine Show and Sale Successful," *Hertford County Herald*, 12 October 1950; "Mrs. Chavis Declared Winner In County-wide Food Contest," *Hertford County Herald*, 7 December 1950.

Clarence Chavis served as the president of the Atlantic District Fair from the 1930s into the 1960s. His organizational affiliations included the Masons and Odd Fellows. He was also a successful farmer and longtime deacon at Pleasant Plains Baptist Church. (Private Collection)

Claudia Hare Chavis was a prize-winning culinary expert. During the mid-twentieth century, she captured numerous awards for cooking and canning at the Atlantic District Fair and state fair. Chavis was also a founding member and chairperson of the deaconess board at Pleasant Plains Baptist Church. (Private Collection)

The 1940 wedding of Dr. Joseph D. Weaver and Alice Saluda Hall was one of the major social highlights in the county. The event, which took place at the home of Hall's mother Mary Saluda Newsome Hall, received coverage in the local media. The marriage united two of the most well-to-do families in the community. Robin Hood Bizzelle, III, Jean Chavis, and Christine Chavis are in the front row. Standing in the second row are J. Basil Weaver, Joseph D. Weaver, Alice Saluda Hall Weaver, Julia Hall, and Edward Hunter. Standing in the third row are Robin Hood Bizzelle, Jr., Clarice Hall Bizzelle, Lyman Lowe, Georgia Hall, Mary Saluda Newsome Hall, and Moses Newsome. (Private Collection)

During the Jim Crow era, descendants of the free people of color held a variety of private events, which allowed them to socialize with friends and family. As in the nineteenth century, weddings continued to be important functions among them. Many couples celebrated their unions with small private gatherings. Large weddings were less common but often received the greatest fanfare. The wedding for Joseph D. Weaver and Alice Saluda Hall was one of the most celebrated ceremonies during the period. Held at the home of the bride's mother Mary Saluda Newsome

126

Hall on August 27, 1940, the wedding included a ceremony with a pastor, groomsmen, and bridesmaids along with a reception. The bride wore a silk and taffeta dress, a string of pearls, and a Juliet cap "held in place by a wreath of pearlized orange blossoms," adornments typically worn by the well-to-do.[179] In contrast to the limited occurrences of large weddings, birthday parties were ordinary occurrences among the descendants of free people of color by the mid-twentieth century. On November 28, 1950, Abscilla "Abbie" Keene Butler's daughters gave their mother a surprise birthday party; the event included gift giving and the serving of refreshments. Family reunions also became important events for descendants of free people of color as social and economic changes such as industrialization and the growth of cities scattered once centralized families across the country. In 1949, the Burke, Green, Reid, Jones, and Rooks families of Hertford and Gates Counties celebrated their second reunion in Murfreesboro. Nancy Ella Hall Reid and her daughter Claudia Reid hosted the grand affair, which included nearly 200 attendees. Family members came together from as far as New York, New Jersey, Ohio, and Arizona to commemorate their heritage.[180]

Although whites often excluded them from the most lucrative business ventures, some descendants of the free people of color discovered entrepreneurial success during the Jim Crow era. J. Eley Reid owned Chowan Beach, a resort for people of color. The beach featured cottages with hot and cold running water, electric lights, and showers, a power plant, a natural spring, merry-go-round, restaurant, and dance pavilion. Willie Manley organized and owned a local Negro League baseball team, the Chowan Bees. Members of the Hall family operated the Casa Mayama, a local nightclub. Joseph D. Weaver's medical practice served the needs of people of color during the segregation era. Descendants of free people of color dominated the funeral home business in the county. The proprietors of Hertford County Undertakers, Reynolds Funeral Home,

---

[179] "Young Doctor Takes Bride In Eastern North Carolina Wedding," *Norfolk Journal and Guide*, 7 December 1940.
[180] "Birthday Party Given Mrs. Butler," *Hertford County Herald*, 7 December 1950; "Carolina Family Has Gala Reunion In Murfreesboro," *Norfolk Journal and Guide*, 10 September 1949.

During the twentieth century, members of the Reynolds family were proprietors of several businesses including Reynolds Funeral Home. Standing from the left are Sarah Reynolds Reid, Etta Reynolds Archer, Minnie Reynolds Manley, Mamie Reynolds Collins, and Amaza Reynolds Faulkner. Seated in the middle from the left are Izola Reynolds Fleming, Spergeon Reynolds, Rufus H. Reynolds, Clarence Reynolds, Brode Reynolds, and Genevieve Reynolds Eason. Fostina Reynolds and Ercles Reynolds are seated in the front. (Private Collection)

and Hunter's Funeral Home were descendants of the county's free people of color. Many of the county's small shopkeepers came from families whose freedom traced back before the end of slavery. Dudley "Erk" Weaver was the proprietor of Weaver Brothers Mercantile Company during the first half of the century. In 1936, Sherwood Jones opened the only grocery store owned and operated by a person of color in Winton at the time. Tupper W. Jones, Talmadge Reid, and Delaware Jones ran stores in Cofield while Dewey Keene and Sheldon Simmons owned establishments on Highway 13. Clarence Reynolds opened a cleaning and tailoring business in Ahoskie. Thomas "Tommie" Boone was the proprietor of a shoe repair shop in Murfreesboro. During the 1930s, Arthur Jones operated a filling station south of Winton. Julius A. Watford owned Watford's Motor Service, an auto garage, in Ahoskie.[181]

---

[181] "Personal," *The Crisis*, November 1915, 222; "Camera Views of Chowan Beach, Popular North Carolina Watering Place," *Norfolk Journal and Guide*, 13 April 1935;

Delaware Jones was one of many members of his family to operate a store. His grocery store was located in the Cofield community and served the needs of locals during the mid-twentieth century. (Private Collection)

Dudley E. Flood and Ben Watford, *You Can't Fall Off The Floor* (Bloomington: AuthorHouse, 2009), 181-189, 201-216; "History & Staff," Hunter's Funeral Home, accessed March 12, 2016, http://www.huntersfuneralhome.com/who-we-are/history-and-staff; "Negro Deaths," *Hertford County Herald*, 10 August 1950; *Ahoskie Era of Hertford County*, 243-250; "Moved in New House," *Hertford County Herald*, 20 July 1950; "Delaware Jones Groceries," "Holiday Memo," *Campus Whisper* (Winton), December 1959; "Murfreesboro," *Norfolk Journal and Guide*, 21 March 1942; "3 Gable Inn," "Watford Motor Co.," *Hertford County Herald*, 23 July 1953.

Madge Watford Hunter (left) and Julius A. Watford (below) were the children of Andrew Watford and Julia Bizzelle Watford. Madge and her husband Howard Hunter were the original proprietors of Hunter's Funeral Home. She was also a teacher. Julius owned Watford's Motor Service. Additionally, Madge and Julius were active in the Hertford County social scene. Madge was a member of the Lady Ambassadors Club, and Julius was a member of the Ambassadors Club. (Private Collection)

Cling L. Pierce, son of Solomon Pierce and Mary Magdalene Hall Pierce, was a prize-winning hog farmer. In 1950, his boar won a top prize at the Atlantic District Fair. (Private Collection)

Throughout the Jim Crow period, agriculture remained a vital part of the Hertford County economy, and descendants of free people of color including some of those with other businesses, relied on agricultural production to feed their families or in some instances expand their wealth. Many of the county's major farmers, especially in the vicinities of Winton, Cofield, Murfreesboro, Union, and Ahoskie, descended from free families. In the 1930s, James H. Sears and Mary Alice Archer Sears maintained a highly reputed poultry farm in the Archertown neighborhood. Through the mid-part of the century, Arthur H. Brett and Cling L. Pierce were prize-winning hog farmers. Although he was a tenant farmer, Floyd Reid was one of the most successful corn producers in the area. Some farmers sought to make extra money by distilling their corn crop and other grains into liquor. Even though bootlegging was an illicit activity, these farmers found the potential profits irresistible, and many ran into trouble with the law for their alleged participation in the production of white lightning and other types of illegal spirits. Beyond farming, many descendants of free people of color made a living as loggers. Watson L. Greene managed a timber cutting business along with his farm. Several members of the Jones family including brothers Willis E. and Walter T. Jones and their sons worked as contractors and laborers in the logging business.[182]

The desire for greater opportunities led many descendants of free people of color to relocate beyond Hertford County during the Jim Crow period. Free people of color and their descendants had migrated in search of greater opportunities since the 1700s, yet the scale of the twentieth

---

[182] "Poultry Farm Report Shows Large Profit," *Norfolk Journal and Guide*, 11 March 1939; "Annual Farm Tour Held in Hertford County, N. C.," *Norfolk Journal and Guide*, 8 April 1939; "Award Winners At Negro Fair Listed By Agent," *Hertford County Herald*, 28 October 1937; "Talmadge Chavis Shows Grand Champion Hog At Atlantic District Fair In Ahoskie," *Hertford County Herald*, 23 October 1951; "Wallace James and Floyd Reid Named Top Corn Growers," *Hertford County Herald*, 30 November 1950; "Wrong Place, Wrong Time: $100 Fine In Liquor Case," *Hertford County Herald*, 21 November 1963; "Dump 300 Gallons of Fermenting Mash In County Raid On Still," *Hertford County Herald*, 22 March 1965; "Archertown," E. Franklin Frazier Papers Box 131-92, Folder 7; Manuscript Division, Moorland-Spingarn Research Center, Howard University; Hertford County Record of Deeds, Volume 52, 344-345; SANC. For names of loggers, see 1940 U. S. Federal Census, Hertford County, North Carolina.

Mary Alice Archer Sears and her husband James H. Sears owned a successful
poultry farming operation in the Archertown community. The Searses produced
chickens and eggs for the market. (Private Collection)

Watson L. Greene and Sarah Elizabeth "Betty" Nickens Greene operated a profitable farm in the Bluefoot Road section of the county. Watson also managed a logging business and was a member of the Masonic lodge in Winton. Hertford County residents remembered the Greenes as one of the first families in their neighborhood to own an electric generator. (Private Collection)

Walter T. Jones (right) and his son James "Jim" Jones (left) were two of several members of the Jones family involved in the logging business. (Private Collection)

century movement would dramatically reshape the social world in the county in ways unlike the previous movements. Some of the greatest accomplishments made by descendants took place beyond the borders of the county.

Descendants who worked in the medical field found great success beyond Hertford County. After graduating from Virginia Union University in 1900, Clinton Caldwell Boone, son of Lemuel Washington Boone and Charlotte Chavis Boone, left the United States to work with the Lott Carey Baptist Foreign Mission Society in the Belgian Congo. He returned to his home country and earned a medical degree from Shaw University before returning to Africa to serve as a missionary in Liberia. Following his stays in Africa, Boone wrote about his experiences in *Congo as I Saw It* and *Liberia as I Know It*. John Lassiter and Martha Turner Lassiter's son Norman Lassiter built a highly successful dental practice in Newport News, Virginia during the first decades of the twentieth century. He attended Lincoln University for his undergraduate education, received his D.D.S. from the dental school at the University of Pennsylvania, and also took coursework at Harvard's dental school. As a dentist and oral surgeon, he served both customers of color and white customers including clients at Hampton Institute and the School for the Deaf, Dumb, and Blind. Lassiter represented the United States at international dental conventions in Europe and helped organize dentists of color within the Old Dominion Dental Association.[183]

In addition, many of Hertford County's most talented descendants of free people of color travelled away from home to work in the education field. In the 1950s, Eff Richard Jones and Annie Walden Jones's son Rudolph Jones rose to the presidency of Fayetteville State Teachers College (Fayetteville State University) in Fayetteville, North Carolina. Thelma Ruth Brett, the daughter of Arthur H. Brett and Julia Pierce Brett, left Hertford County for school and completed her education by earning

---

[183] C. C. Boone, *Congo as I Saw It* (New York: J. J. Little and Ives Company, 1927); C. C. Boone, *Liberia as I Know It* (Richmond, 1929), ix; A. B. Caldwell, *History of the American Negro Virginia Edition* (Atlanta: A. B. Caldwell Publishing Company, 1921), 446-448.

Clinton Caldwell Boone, son of Lemuel Washington Boone and Charlotte Chavis Boone, was a doctor and active missionary during the early twentieth century. He was the author of *Congo as I Saw It* and *Liberia as I Know It*. (Private Collection)

Thelma Ruth Brett, better known as Ruth, received her doctorate from Columbia University in 1945. Her career as an educator included stints at Tuskegee Institute, Spellman College, Bennett College, Dillard University, and Morgan State University. After finishing her doctorate, she married the noted historian Benjamin Quarles. (Private Collection)

her doctorate from Columbia University. Brett taught and worked in the administrations of several centers of higher education including Tuskegee Institute, Spellman College, Bennett College, Dillard University, and Morgan State University.[184]

Hobson Reynolds, the son of Rufus H. Reynolds and Julia Keene Reynolds, discovered several uncommon opportunities beyond Hertford County and made a name for himself hundreds of miles from home. In the 1920s, he opened an undertaking establishment in Philadelphia, Pennsylvania. While living there, he became interested in politics and won a seat in the state legislature. Later in his life, Reynolds held the title of the Grand Exalted Ruler of the Improved Benevolent Protective Order of Elks of the World, overseeing more than half a million members.[185]

The accomplishments of some descendants of free people of color highlight the importance of wealth among the larger number of descendants. Access to wealth played a significant role in defining the opportunities available to this population during the Jim Crow era. The most well-to-do families enjoyed many luxuries and privileges unavailable to their poorer neighbors. Before the establishment of a complete primary and secondary educational system, access to wealth largely defined who would and would not finish high school. Even after the county started to run public secondary schools for children of color, those children who came from families who could spare them from the farm were the ones most likely to finish high school. Well-to-do families tended to have the best living situations; they owned their homes and could decorate them with the most up-to-date fixtures. When electric lights became available, they were the first to acquire them, and the same patterned followed for indoor plumbing. A few individuals owned items that would have been extravagant for anyone of their time. W. D. Newsome and Norman Hall

---

[184] "Winton Graduate Is Dean of Women," *Hertford County Herald*, 8 September 1938; "Dean at Bennett," *Norfolk Journal and Guide*, 5 September 1942; "Earns Doctorate," *The Pittsburgh Courier*, 8 September 1945; "College and School News," *The Crisis*, March 1957, 179-183.

[185] "Eve Lynn Chats 'Bout Society and Folks," *Pittsburgh Courier*, 18 October 1924; "Hobson Reynolds At 'Y' Sunday," *Pittsburgh Courier*, 12 October 1935; "Rheingold Salutes A Good Neighbor...Hobson R. Reynolds," *Ebony*, September 1961, 93.

both kept significant life insurance policies, which passed on to their heirs after their deaths. Newsome, along with Louisiana Weaver Hall, who both lived into the 1910s, had significant holdings in financial securities. Joseph D. Weaver, the community doctor, owned an airplane and a private landing field.[186]

Although the advantages of the pre-Civil War period helped several individuals succeed during Jim Crow times, other descendants of free people of color were not so fortunate. As in past periods, lack of resources prevented many individuals from reaching their full potential. The local colored schools often had troubles with enrollments because every child of color was not able to attend school. Some children worked instead of attending school. There were many poor land owners among the less fortunate but the landless made up the lowest caste in the community. Circumstances forced these people to do menial labor or sharecrop, often under less than optimal conditions. It was not uncommon for poor descendants of free people of color to work for the more well-to-do descendants on their farms and in their business operations.[187]

The legal regime that upheld Jim Crow in Hertford County and other parts of the United States started to crumble in the 1950s and 1960s. Some descendants of free people of color, like their Reconstruction-period forbearers, would discover opportunity in the new age. By 1950, they along with other people of color began to organize. Under the leadership of Solomon Keene, people of color formed the Democratic Negro Voters' Club of Hertford County. In the April 20, 1950 issue of the *Hertford County Herald*, Keene posted an advertisement for the first meeting of the organization. Keene told the local newspaper that goal of the group was "to get the eligible Negro voters to the polls."[188] He used the newspaper to draw interest to the club, and an advertisement for the group appeared in the May 18, 1950 edition of the *Hertford County Herald*. In the

---

[186] Hertford County Record of Wills, Volume D, 324-326, 380-384, SANC; Hertford County Record of Wills, Volume E, 260-268, SANC; "Dr. Weaver Moves Into New Residence," *Hertford County Herald*, 20 July 1950.
[187] Flood and Watford, *You Can't Fall Off The Floor*, 217-219.
[188] "Mass Meeting Held," *Hertford County Herald*, 20 April 1950; "Keene Explains Negro Voters' Club Efforts," *Hertford County Herald*, 16 May 1950.

Solomon Keene led the Democratic Negro Voters' Club of Hertford County during the early 1950s. The club encouraged eligible people of color to vote. Keene also served as a delegate to the Hertford County Democratic Convention and was Grand Orator of the Masons in North Carolina. (Private Collection)

Bessie Keene Hall (center) was active in a variety of political, social, and educational efforts. Along with her brother Solomon Keene, Hall served as a delegate to the Hertford County Democratic Convention in 1950 and participated in the Democratic Negro Voters' Club of Hertford County. She was a teacher and an officer in the C. S. Brown School PTA. Hall was also active in several organizations within Pleasant Plains Baptist Church and served as the president of the Pleasant Plains Home Demonstration Club. She is pictured with her granddaughter Peggy Smallwood DeBerry (left) and her daughter Elsie Hall Smallwood (right). (Private Collection)

advertisement, Keene stated, "All Negro Democrats are asked to be present at The Elk Home in Ahoskie at 3 o'clock, Sunday, May 21, for a pre-election rally."[189] At the Elks' Home, he planned to hold a discussion about the various Democratic candidates running for office. Only a few days earlier, Keene, along with his sister Bessie Keene Hall, attended the Hertford County Democratic Convention. The siblings attended the convention as delegates representing the Winton precinct. The *Hertford County Herald* reported that their attendance at the convention was the "first time in the memory of those present" that "two Negroes attended a Hertford County Democratic Convention and were recognized as delegates."[190] Keene and his organization opened the doors for serious changes in local politics.

Descendants of free people of color through organizations such as the National Association for the Advancement of Colored People (NAACP) strived to bring Hertford County out of the troubling times of the Jim Crow era. Collis Brown, a descendant, along with John Scott, led the NAACP during the early 1960s. When the Ahoskie Good Neighbor Committee, a group tasked with minimizing conflicts between people of color and whites, failed to adequately fulfill their mission, the NAACP pressed them to improve. In 1965, the organization's leadership pressured the county's board of education to permit integration of the schools. Thirty-one parents and 58 children sent a petition to the board requesting that students, teachers, and other staff have access to the "school which they would be initially assigned if white."[191]

Through the efforts of various organizations in Hertford County along with changes in state and federal policy, a new sociopolitical situation began to take shape by the 1960s. Descendants of free people of color ran for public office, and in 1963, J. Eley Reid and Sheldon Simmons made news headlines after declaring their intent to seek seats on Winton's town council. Both men lost in the election that year, but eventually became

---

[189] "Notice," *Hertford County Herald*, 18 May 1950.
[190] "Negroes Attend Convention Health Contest," *Hertford County Herald*, 9 May 1950.
[191] "Racial Conflict May Heat Again: Brown," *Hertford County Herald*, 13 February 1964; "Board Discusses Negro Petition," *Hertford County Herald*, 5 April 1965.

During the 1960s, Collis Brown served as the president of the Hertford County branch of the National Association for the Advancement of Colored People (NAACP). He was an important proponent of school integration in the county. (Private Collection)

J. Eley Reid was the proprietor of the Chowan Beach resort and owner of several other businesses. In many ways, Reid followed in the footsteps of his grandfather Eli Williamson, who was a farmer and distillery owner in the late nineteenth century. Upon taking a seat on the Winton Town Council in 1963, Reid was among the first people of color to hold public office since the Reconstruction period. He was also the treasurer and manager of the Atlantic District Fair. (Private Collection)

councilmen after deaths and resignations opened positions within the body. By 1964, both Reid and Simmons participated in the governance of the town. After the passage of federal civil rights legislation, Hertford County leaders initiated a process to permit children of color to attend the schools originally designated for white pupils. The first group of students of color enrolled in the traditionally white schools under the freedom of choice plan in fall of 1965.[192]

The Jim Crow period can be viewed as both "the best of times and the worst of times" for descendants of Hertford County's free people of color. During the period, many of them took advantage of educational and economic opportunities unavailable to their forbearers, and within the space reserved for them, many individuals flourished. Yet the impacts of the Jim Crow system and the white people who created and supported inequality and discrimination should not be underestimated. Violence, although rare, was a key feature of the Jim Crow system. The development of segregated spaces and organizations transformed society in ways unknown before certain white people instituted Jim Crow customs. Many forms of interaction that existed between people of color and whites before the twentieth century nearly disappeared with the institution of segregationists' policies. The practices of Jim Crow created fractures in intimacy and trust that people are still trying to repair.

---

[192] "Reid Files For Winton Council," *Hertford County Herald*, 16 April 1963; "Two Negroes In Race: Winton Election Slate Complete for May 7," *Hertford County Herald*, 18 April 1963; "Two Seek Council Seats in Winton, NC," *Norfolk Journal and Guide*, 27 August 1963; "N. C. Town Gets 2nd Negro On 5-Man Council," *Norfolk Journal and Guide*, 11 April 1964; "County School Board Approves Plan To Comply With '64 Civil Rights Act," *Hertford County Herald*, 1 March 1965; "Board Discusses Negro Petition," *Hertford County Herald*, 5 April 1965.

# Conclusion

The stories of Hertford County's free people of color and their descendants are constantly evolving narratives. Although no longer a place in its economic high point, Hertford County is the site of a rich history and future potential. Many of the county's political and business leaders come from the families of color who were free before the Civil War. Beyond Hertford County, descendants of the county's free people of color have made numerous accomplishments as there are many doctors, lawyers, politicians, scholars, business owners, military veterans, and organizational leaders among their numbers. Of course many of the descendants of the free people of color are also among those who do the most backbreaking work or live under the most troubling conditions.

The inheritance of the descendants of Hertford County's free people of color is great and yet the value attached to that bequest is mixed. Numerous families continue to hold on to the legacies of their free ancestors of color as some still retain the properties held by those ancestors. Other descendants hang pictures from their walls or care for family cemeteries in order to preserve the memories of those who came before them. Nevertheless, there are many descendants who know neither their ancestors names nor their stories. I hope this book will partially remedy that situation.

# Appendix 1

Surnames of Hertford County's Free People of Color

Adkins, Allen, Archer, Artis, Askew, Bailey, Baker, Banks, Bass, Bateman, Benton, Best, Berry, Bird, Bizzell, Boone, Bowens, Bowser, Britt, Brown, Butler, Carey, Carr, Catus, Chavis, Collins, Cone, Copeland, Cotton, Crawford, Cuff, Cumbo, Davis, Dolby, Doughtie, Dunston, Edge, Ely, Ellis, Flood, Freeman, Garnes, Gee, Gibbs, Green, Haithcock, Hall, Hicks, Hunt, Huson, Huss, Jenkins, Jones, Jordan, Keene, King, Lamb, Lang, Lashley, Lassiter, Lawrence, Lee, Lewis, Luton, Manley, Manning, Matthews, Melton, Mitchell, Morris, Newsome, Nickens, Orange, Overton, Parker, Pierce, Pugh, Reid, Reynolds, Ricks, Robbins, Roberts, Saunders, Sawyer, Scott, Sears, Shepherd, Shoecraft, Simmons, Smith, Smothers, Spiers, Stafford, Stuart, Tann, Thomas, Trummell, Turner, Walden, Weaver, Wiggins, Williams, Williamson, Woodson, Wyatt, Yates

# Appendix 2

Petition of coloured persons to the Legislature [1822]

To the Honorable the General Assembly of the State of North Carolina.

Your petitioners coloured persons citizens of this State would approach your Honorable Body with all the difference & respect due to the Character of Representatives of the People

They beg leave to state that some of them whose names are affixed to this petition bore an honorable part in the seven years war which established the Liberties of their Common Country: That during that eventful period they were taught to believe that all men are by nature free & equal, and that the enjoyment of life, liberty and property aught to be secured alike to every Citizen without exception & without distinction.

With these views they need not
attempt

149

attempt to express to your Honorable Body the deep Concern with which they learned of the passage of a Law at the last Session of the Legislature by which their lives & liberties are virtually placed at the mercy of Slaves. They would ask of your Honorable Body whether their situation ever before the Revolution was not preferable to one in which their dearest rights are held by so slight a tenure as the favour of Slaves and the will & caprice of their vindictive masters: for it cannot escape the notice of your Honorable Body that persons of this description are bound to a blind obedience, and know no Law, but the will of their masters—

Your petitioners will not believe that your Honorable Body will hesitate to lend a compassionate ear to their well grounded complaints

complaints, and to redress a grievance so oppressive to them, and so wholly incongenial with the spirit of our republican government.

They therefore humbly pray your Honorable Body that the Act of the last session of the Legislature making slaves competent witnesses against them in criminal cases may be repealed.

Allen Brown
John + Raniel

William Brown Sen
William Smith
James Smith
John Stafford
Wesley W Lee
William Weaver
Wiley Cotton

Lawrence Weaver
Rich Cotton
Elias + Weaver
   his
   mark

Deanel Jones
Moses Manly

Dempsey + Edward
John Season
Briton Read
Jesse Weaver
James Reynolds
John Buzzell
Allen Hall

Orren Wyatt

Kinston Rollins
William Manly

151

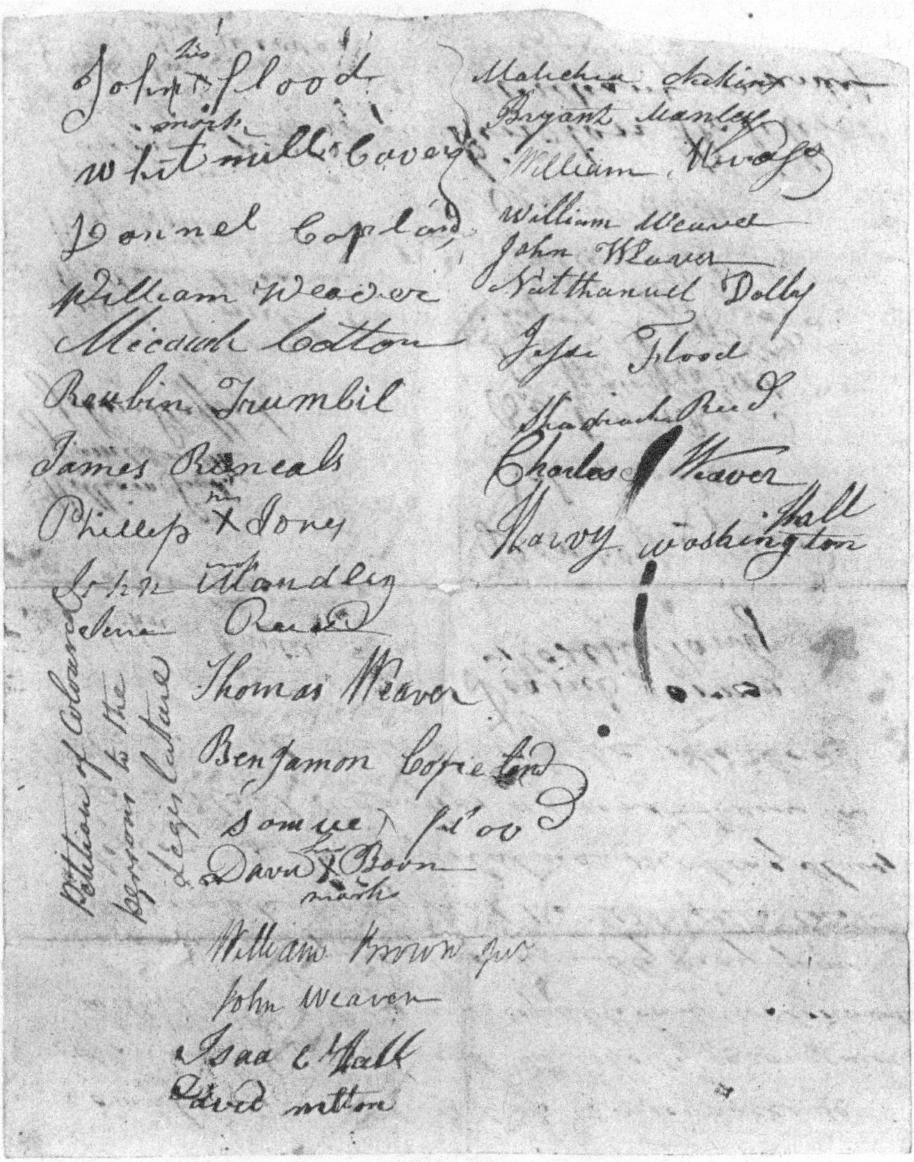

John Flood
his mark

whit mill Cavey

Dannel Copland

william Weaver

Micdaah Cotton

Reubin Trumbil

James Reneals

Phillep + Jones
his mark

John Handley

Jesse Reed

Thomas Weaver

Benjamon Copieland

Samuel Flood

David + Boon
mark

William Brown Jur.

John Weaver

Isaac Hall

David milton

Malechia Jekins

Bryant Manley

William Weaver

William Weaver

John Weaver

Natthanuel Dolby

Jesse Flood

Shadrach Reed

Charles Weaver

Harvy Woshington Hall

Petition of Colored persons to the legislature

152

# Index

154

Garnes, Celia, 29
Garnes, Daniel, 35, 102, 151
Garnes, Gabrilla Branson, 115
Garnes, Mollie, 76, 77
Garnes, Wiley, 48
Garnes, Winborn, 24
Garnes Family, 6, 23, 102
Garrett, Ardelle, 108, 112, 113, 115, 118
Gates County, North Carolina, 24, 26, 79, 127
Gatling, Lala Wilson, 120
Gee, London, 31
Gibbs, Lucy, 26
Giles, Osborn A., 64
Glee Club, 108, 114
Godwin, Barnaby, 12
Goldsboro, North Carolina, 74
Grandfather Clause, 97, 102, 105, 107
Grant, Ulysses, 64, 66
Green, Nancy Smothers, 19
Green, Smith, 30, 41, 48, 72
Greene, Sarah Elizabeth Nickens, 134
Greene, Watson L., 132, 134
Greensboro, North Carolina, 111
Haithcock Family, 31
Hall, Albert Valentine, 75
Hall, Albina Sears, 120
Hall, Alice Saluda, 126
Hall, Albert, 103
Hall, Allen, 16, 37, 44, 76, 102, 103, 149
Hall, Andrew, 17, 44, 76
Hall, Bessie Keene, 108, 112, 114, 118, 121, 142, 143
Hall, Crawleigh Finney, 105
Hall, Delno, 75
Hall, Dicie, 112. *See also* Dicie Hall Reid
Hall, Elizabeth Manley, 120
Hall, Harvey, 16, 46, 76, 150
Hall, Harvey Washington, 152
Hall, Isaac, 152
Hall, Joseph, 6, 8, 30
Hall, Lavenia, 85
Hall, Louisa Butler, 88
Hall, Margaret, 7

Hall, Margaret "Peggy," 16, 44
Hall, Marmaduke, 88, 92
Hall, Mary Saluda Newsome, 126
Hall, Mollie Cherry, 28
Hall, Norman, 107, 108, 139
Hall, Preston, 48, 76, 102
Hall, Sherman P., 118
Hall, Thelma Susan Jones, 120
Hall, Viola, 112. *See also* Viola Hall Chavis
Hall, Virginia S., 85, 88
Hall, Wells, 105
Hall, William, 17, 18, 32, 41, 102, 103, 118
Hall, William James, 102, 105, 108, 116
Hampton Institute, 16, 80, 82, 84, 86, 87, 95, 136
Hampton, Virginia, 86, 88, 95
Hampton Roads, Virginia, 7
Hare, Fannie Jones, 116
Harrell, Starkey S., 19
Harrison, Henry, 77
Harvard University, 136
Hertford County Herald, 98, 140, 143
Hertford County Home Demonstration Club, 121
Hertford County Training School, 99
Hertford County Undertakers, 117, 127
Hoggard, Thomas, 32
Holly, Baccus, 34
Howard, John Lazarus, 19
Howard, Mary Brown, 19
Hunt, John, 48
Hunter, Edward, 126
Hunter, Howard, 130
Hunter, Madge Watford, 130
Hunter, Peter, 59
Hunter, Preston, 103
Hunter's Funeral Home, 128
Indiana, 22, 23
Jackson, North Carolina, 62
Jacksonville, Florida, 58
James, Wallace, 111
Jenkins, Texanna Jones, 40, 116
Jernigan, Lemuel R., 41, 44, 53
Jernigan, Miles H., 42
Jones, Albert, 40

156

Manley, Eunice Downing, 120
Manley, Gabriel, 6, 8, 10, 12
Manley, George D., 69
Manley, J. D., 81
Manley, John, 152
Manley, Jesse, 36, 37
Manley, Lemuel M., 108
Manley, Littleton, 6
Manley, Mark, 12
Manley, Moses, 151
Manley, Moses, Jr., 12
Manley, Minnie, 128
Manley, Parthena, 34
Manley, Penelope, 34
Manley, Preston D., 69
Manley, Rachel, 41
Manley, Solomon, 12
Manley, William, 151
Manley, Willis, 17
Manley, Wilson, 60
Masons, 107, 116, 117, 141
McPherson, James, 31
Meherrin Baptist Church, 31, 77
Melton, Abner J., 116
Melton, Anderson, 102
Melton, Ashley, 72
Melton, Calcey D., 71
Melton, David, 46, 152
Melton, Feraby, 39
Melton, Lewis, 48
Melton, Lovey, 46
Melton, Marina, 46
Melton, Martha, 46
Melton, Mary Frances, 19
Melton, Meady, 34, 48, 72
Melton, Mills, 72
Melton, Nellie Gray Manley, 121
Melton, Rebecca, 71
Melton, Richard P., 71
Melton, Susan Jones, 40
Melton, Wiley, 71
Melton Family, 23, 31, 102
Michigan, 22, 23
Mill Neck Baptist Church, 79
Mitchell, Allen, 26
Mitchell, Horatio, 75
Mitchell, Miles, 53

Mitchell, Polly Gibbs, 25, 26
Mitchell Family, 92
Mizzell, Joseph A., 32
Modlin, Henry, 32
Morgan State University, 138, 139
Morris, Mac, 48
Morris, William, 152
Mount Tabor Baptist Church, 31
Mountain, Cado, 95
Murfreesboro, North Carolina, 4, 26,
34, 43, 64, 66, 67, 85, 88, 127, 128, 134
Nansemond County, Virginia, 59
New Ahoskie Baptist Church, 79, 109,
115
New Bern, North Carolina, 55, 57, 58,
60, 61
New Farmers of America (NFA), 111,
112
New Homemakers of America (NHA),
111
New Hope Baptist Church, 79
New Jersey, 127
New York, 56, 127
Newport News, Virginia, 136
Newsome, Dempsey, 17, 60, 61
Newsome, Elizabeth "Betsey" Manley,
17, 20, 61
Newsome, Martha, 60, 61
Newsome, Moses, 126
Newsome, William David (W. D.), 41,
64, 66, 68, 74, 79, 85, 98, 139
Newsome Family, 92
Newsome Grove Baptist Church, 77,
115, 116
Nickens, Alice Jones, 120. *See also*
Alice Jones Scott
Nickens, Bessie Gilligan, 56, 106
Nickens, Boone, 19, 30
Nickens, Carter, 12
Nickens, Edward, 12
Nickens, Henry, 44, 47
Nickens, Hilary, 42
Nickens, James, 6, 10, 12
Nickens, James Henry, 69
Nickens, Joshua, 56, 57, 92, 106
Nickens, Malachi, 12, 13, 152
Nickens, Martha Susan, 91

159

161

Warren Eugene Milteer, Jr. is an assistant professor of history at the University of South Carolina and a descendant of Hertford County's free people of color. He received his PhD from the University of North Carolina at Chapel Hill. His publications include articles in the *Journal of Social History* and *North Carolina Historical Review*. He is the recipient of numerous honors including the Historical Society of North Carolina's 2014 R. D. W. Connor Award for the best journal article in the *North Carolina Historical Review*.

Made in the USA
Columbia, SC
25 July 2020

14592518R00095